# Land Policy
# in Modern Indonesia

Books from the Lincoln Institute of Land Policy/OG&H

Land Acquisition in Developing Countries
Michael G. Kitay

Introduction to Computer Assisted Valuation
Edited by Arlo Woolery and Sharon Shea

Second World Congress on Land Policy, 1983
Edited by Matthew Cullen and Sharon Woolery

The Zoning Game Revisited
Richard F. Babcock and Charles L. Siemon

Advanced Industrial Development
Donald Hicks

Land Markets and Land Policy in a Metropolitan Area:
A Case Study of Tokyo
Yuzuru Hanayama

The Urban Caldron
Edited by Joseph DiMento, LeRoy Graymer, and Frank Schnidman

Land Readjustment: The Japanese System
Luciano Minerbi, Peter Nakamura, Kiyoko Nitz, and Jane Yanai

Measuring Fiscal Capacity
Edited by H. Clyde Reeves

Economics and Tax Policy
Karl E. Case

1984 Real Estate Valuation Colloquium:
A Redefinition of Real Estate Appraisal Precepts and Processes
Edited by William N. Kinnard, Jr.

Planning with the Small Computer
Edited by Matthew MacIver and Jan Schreiber

Land Supply Monitoring
David R. Godschalk, Scott A. Bollens, John S. Hekman,
and Mike E. Miles

# Land Policy in Modern Indonesia

## A Study of Land Issues in the New Order Period

Colin MacAndrews

A Lincoln Institute of Land Policy Book

Published by
Oelgeschlager, Gunn & Hain
in association with the
Lincoln Institute of Land Policy

Copyright © 1986 by Oelgeschlager, Gunn & Hain, Publishers, Inc. All rights reserved. No part of this publication may be reproduced or transmitted in any form or by any means, electronic or mechanical (including photocopying and recording), or by any information storage or retrieval system, without the prior written consent of the publisher.

International Standard Book Number: 0-89946-214-6

Library of Congress Catalog Card Number: 86-5144

Printed in the U.S.A.

Oelgeschlager, Gunn & Hain, Publishers, Inc.
131 Clarendon Street
Boston, MA 02116 U.S.A.

**Library of Congress Cataloging in Publication Data**

MacAndrews, Colin.
    Land policy in modern Indonesia.

    "A Lincoln Institute of Land Policy book."
    Bibliography: p.
    Includes index.
    1. Land use—Government policy—Indonesia.
2. Land tenure—Indonesia.    I. Lincoln Institute of Land Policy.    II. Title.
HD893.M33 1986    333.73'09598    86-5144
ISBN 0-89946-214-6

# Contents

# List of Figures and Tables

# Lincoln Institute Foreword

The Lincoln Institute of Land Policy is an educational institute dedicated to the development and exchange of ideas and information pertaining to land policy and property taxation. It is a school offering opportunities for instruction and research. It welcomes government officials, working practitioners, and students to the pursuit of advanced studies.

The Lincoln Institute is also a center for linking the university and the practice of government; for bringing together scholars, professionals, and officials; and for blending the theory and practice of land policy. Each year the Lincoln Institute offers a limited number of fellowships to postdoctoral researchers who propose a program of research and study in the land or tax policy field, and the result of this research is considered for publication in either our monograph or book series.

Dr. Colin MacAndrews was awarded a fellowship to research modern land policy issues in Indonesia. His research was undertaken both in Cambridge and in Indonesia and was under the supervision of Mr. Sein Lin, Director of International and Special Programs at the Lincoln Institute. This book examines the recent history of land policy in Indonesia and serves both as a basic reference text and as a suggested blueprint for new policy initiatives.

The Lincoln Institute publishes this book to provide a resource for scholars, government officials, and landowners in Indonesia and elsewhere and to serve as training material to further the knowledge, understanding, and performance of professionals in the field.

FRANK SCHNIDMAN
*Senior Fellow*

# Preface

The study for *Land Policy in Modern Indonesia* had its origins in the work done at the University of Gadjah Mada between 1976 and 1979, when I was a Rockefeller Foundation staff member involved in a variety of research projects with the Institute for Rural and Regional Studies. One result from that work was an annotated bibliography of land affairs in Indonesia (1978) that laid the foundation for this present study. Little had been published on land affairs in Indonesia at that time, particularly from the point of view of land policy since the 1960s, and this bibliography was an attempt to reopen that particular area of studies to researchers.

In 1983 I was fortunate to be given a fellowship by the Lincoln Institute of Land Policy in Cambridge, Massachusetts, to extend this initial work by looking specifically at the formulation of a national land policy applicable to modern-day Indonesia. Much had changed in Indonesia since the 1960s, and it seemed necessary to examine these changes in terms of land policy. This study is derived from the time spent in Cambridge and from follow-up work I did in Indonesia.

I am grateful to a number of people who helped me in this study. First and foremost to my colleagues and coworkers at the University of Gadjah Mada who initially stimulated my interest in this area. Then to the Lincoln Institute of Land Policy for its support in helping me put together this study and in particular to the Director of International Programmes, Mr. Sein Lin. My thanks are also due to the Massachusetts Institute of Technology's Center for International Studies, which provided me with office space and facilities during my stay in Cambridge.

I of course take full responsibility for all opinions and statements in this book.

# Introduction

## *Currency*

In December 1965 a major currency reform was announced so that 1,000 old rupiahs became equal to 1 new rupiah. Unless otherwise noted, all rupiah (Rp) units used in this book are in new rupiah. Since then there have been a number of devaluations with the foreign exchange rate of the rupiah to the U.S. dollar, changing as follows:

| Year | Rupiah | Year | Rupiah | Year | Rupiah |
|------|--------|------|--------|------|--------|
| 1966 | 235 | 1971 | 415 | 1976 | 415 |
| 1967 | 235 | 1972 | 415 | 1977 | 415 |
| 1968 | 326 | 1973 | 415 | 1978 | 615 |
| 1969 | 326 | 1974 | 415 | 1983 | 785 |
| 1970 | 378 | 1975 | 415 | 1984 | 970[a] |

[a]The rupiah was allowed to float in 1984 and 1985 at an exchange rate to the U.S. dollars between Rp1,050 and Rp 1,120.

## *Financial Years*

Until 1969, financial years covered the same period as calendar years. Beginning in April 1969 (January–March 1969 was a transitional quarter), the financial year was changed to cover the period from April 1 to March 30 the following year; thus, a period shown as 1972/1973 in the text refers to the period between April 1, 1972, to March 30, 1973.

## Statistics

Many statistical series in Indonesia are unreliable. Two figures from the different sources that supposedly refer to the same magnitude often vary by as much as 50 percent. Total land area for instance is quoted at between 1,919 million square kilometers in one set of official statistics and 2,000 million square kilometers or more in other references. Although all possible care has been taken to check sources and correct for errors, all statistical data presented in this book should be interpreted with considerable care.

# 1

## Land in Indonesia

### *Physical Characteristics*

#### *Dimensions*

The land area of Indonesia, 1.92 million kilometers, is spread over 13,667 islands in an archipelago that stretches 5,110 kilometers from west to east and 1,888 kilometers from north to south (Figure 1.1). Of these islands the largest is Kalimantan, followed by Sumatra, Irian Jaya, Sulawesi, and Java (Table 1.1). Of the other islands only 6.8 percent are populated, and more than 55 percent even today remain unnamed (Indonesia, Bureau of Statistics 1982, p. XLV).

#### *Climate*

Climatically, Indonesia, lying on the equator, has a tropical climate although due to its vast size and topographical disparities, there are some differences among areas in both temperature and humidity. The average temperatures range from 22°C in the cold mountain areas to 27°C in the hot coastal zones, with humidity everywhere averaging around 80 percent. The country has two distinct seasons: a dry season from June to September, which is influenced by the Australian continental air masses, and a rainy season from December to March, which is influenced by the Asian continental and Pacific Ocean air masses. Certain areas, however, have rainy seasons almost the whole year, while some areas, such as Central Maluku in Eastern Indonesia, have a completely opposite season, with a rainy season from June to September and a dry season from December to March. The amount of precipitation typically shows a decline as one moves toward the southern and eastern parts of the island chain. Thus, areas in Kalimantan and Sumatra receive a higher rainfall than Java, with much drier conditions found in the Eastern Nusa Tenggara islands. Eastern Indonesia is distinct in having extreme seasons in comparison with much of the rest of the country, with a long dry season from March to October with some rain coming in with the Australian trade winds in June and July and then very heavy monsoon-type rainfall from November through February. This variation in climate has led to the division of the country into what are termed *critical* and *noncritical* areas based on topographical and climatic features, with some 30 percent of the country being categorized as ecologically critical due to the extreme conditions.

*Terrain*

Soils vary among different parts of the country. Areas with extensive volcanic activities, such as Java, have rich alluvial soils that support intensive agriculture in comparison to the far larger outer island areas where the soils are very poor. While both detailed land use and soil surveys are lacking,[1] the country can be divided into three distinct major terrain patterns: (1) mountainous land (mainly lithosols and andosols), defined by the 200 meter contour that accounts for 41 percent of Indonesia's total land area; (2) level or undulating to hilly land (mainly red-yellow podzolics, ferralsols, red-brown Mediterranean soils, and regosols), which accounts for 32 percent of the total land area; and (3) swampy lands (mainly organic soils and alluvials), which accounts for 27 percent of total land area (Table 1.2). A large part of Sulawesi (69 percent of total land area) and Kalimantan (41 percent of total land area) falls within the first category, whereas 59 percent of the land area in Nusa Tenggara and Maluku is in the second category. In Java, Bali, and Madura and Sumatra, the three terrain types can be found in roughly equal proportions.

## Land-use Patterns

How much of Indonesia's terrain is suitable for agricultural purposes is unclear because of inadequate data and mapping, but estimates place the figure at about 60 million hectares from the total land area of some 200 million hectares. Of this, 17 million hectares are already under cultivation, leaving over 40 million hectares of potentially cultivable land remaining to come under cultivation, mainly in Sumatra and Kalimantan (see Table 1.2).

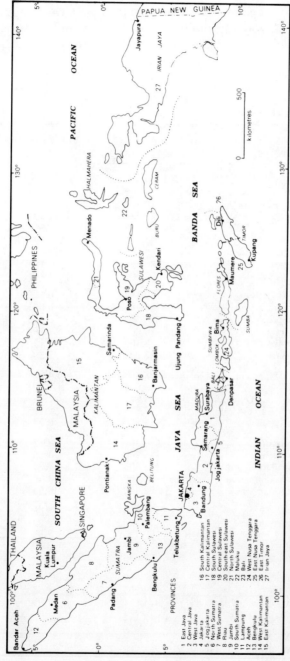

Figure 1.1. Map of Indonesia

In terms of agriculture land use, Indonesia is characterized by two major agricultural patterns derived from the country's ecological conditions and population distribution. On the small island of Java, in which in 1980 approximately 62 percent of the country's population was

**Table 1.1**
**Land Area in Indonesia**

| Province | Area (square kilometers) | Percent of Total Area of Indonesia |
|---|---|---|
| Sumatra | 473,606 | 24.67 |
| Aceh | 55,392 | 2.88 |
| North Sumatra | 70,787 | 3.69 |
| West Sumatra | 49,778 | 2.59 |
| Riau | 94,562 | 4.93 |
| Jambi | 44,924 | 2.34 |
| South Sumatra | 103,688 | 5.40 |
| Bengkulu | 21,168 | 1.10 |
| Lampung | 33,307 | 1.74 |
| Java and Madura | 132,187 | 6.89 |
| Jakarta | 590 | 0.03 |
| West Java | 46,300 | 2.41 |
| Central Java | 34,206 | 1.78 |
| Yogyakarta | 3,169 | 0.17 |
| East Java | 47,992 | 2.50 |
| Bali and Nusa Tenggara | 88,488 | 4.61 |
| Bali | 5,561 | 0.29 |
| West Nusa Tenggara | 20,177 | 1.05 |
| East Nusa Tenggara | 47,876 | 2.49 |
| East Timor | 14,874 | 0.78 |
| Kalimantan | 539,460 | 28.11 |
| West Kalimantan | 146,740 | 7.65 |
| Central Kalimantan | 152,600 | 7.95 |
| South Kalimantan | 37,660 | 1.96 |
| East Kalimantan | 202,440 | 10.55 |
| Sulawesi | 189,216 | 9.85 |
| North Sulawesi | 19,023 | 0.99 |
| Central Sulawesi | 69,726 | 3.63 |
| South Sulawesi | 72,781 | 3.79 |
| Southeast Sulawesi | 27,686 | 1.44 |
| Maluku and Irian Jaya | 496,486 | 25.87 |
| Maluku | 74,505 | 3.88 |
| Irian Jaya | 421,981 | 21.99 |
| Total | 1,919,443 | 100 |

*Source:* Indonesia, Bureau of Statistics (1982).

**Table 1.2.**
**Land Area by Region: Agricultural Potential and Type of Terrain/Soil Group**
(million of hectares)

| Province | Group 1[a] | | Group 2[b] | | Group 3[c] | | Total | |
|---|---|---|---|---|---|---|---|---|
| | Total Area % | with Agri. Potential % | Total Area % | with Agri. Potential % | Total Area % | with Agri. Potential % | Total Area % | with Agri. Potential % |
| Java, Madura and Bali | 5.3 (38) | 1.1 (20) | 4.1 (29) | 3.2 (80) | 4.6 (33) | 3.7 (80) | 14.0 (100) | 8.0 (57) |
| Sumatra | 16.4 (32) | 3.3 (20) | 17.7 (34) | 14.2 (80) | 17.9 (34) | 1.8 (10) | 52.0 (100) | 19.3 (37) |
| Kalimantan | 22.3 (41) | 2.2 (10) | 14.0 (25) | 11.2 (80) | 18.7 (34) | 3.7 (20) | 55.0 (100) | 17.1 (31) |
| Sulawesi | 15.8 (69) | 1.6 (10) | 5.4 (23) | 4.3 (80) | 1.8 (8) | 1.1 (60) | 23.0 (100) | 7.0 (31) |
| Nusa Tenggara and Maluku | 5.7 (38) | 0.6 (10) | 8.8 (59) | 7.1 (80) | 0.5 (3) | 0.2 (50) | 15.0 (100) | 7.9 (52) |
| Indonesia (Total)[d] | 65.5 (41) | 8.8 (13) | 50.0 (32) | 40.0 (80) | 43.5 (27) | 10.5 (25) | 159.0 (100) | 59.3 (37) |

*Source:* Bureau of Statistics, *Statistical Year Book* (1971), p. 3.

*Note:* [a] Group 1: Mountainous land, mainly lithosols and andosols.
[b] Group 2: Level or undulating to hilly land, mainly red-yellow podzolics, ferrasols, red-brown Mediterranean soils and regosols.
[c] Group 3: Swampy lands, mainly organic soils and alluvials.
[d] Excluding 41.0 million hectares in Irian Jaya.

living,[2] one finds intensive land use based on irrigated and rain-fed wet rice cultivation. These features, allied with the very favorable climatological and geological conditions, help give Java, although it represents only 6.9 percent the country's total land area, a dominant role in the agricultural life of the country. Seventy percent of the cultivable land in Java is cultivated year round, and its intensive type of cultivation stands in marked contrast to the more extensive dry land, or swidden, type of cultivation found in most of the outer island areas.

The swidden agricultural system involves clearing the forested areas and subjecting the land to a cycle of intermittent cultivation interspersed with much longer fallow periods when the soil is allowed to recover its natural fertility. The cropping regimen in a particular swidden plot is usually quite diverse and can involve the intercropping of more than a dozen cultigens such as dry rice, cassava, gourds, maize, yams, and a wide range of other vegetables and fruits. Swidden culture involves both commercial and subsistence features. Hudson, for instance, based on work in Kalimantan, has noted that:

> [I]n almost all areas where it is practiced, the swidden horticultural system serves as only one strand in a multiplex socio-economic system that has both subsistence and cash components. The subsistence component involves not only the products of horticulture, but of fishing, hunting, and the gathering of such commodities as rubber, rattan, and timber, but could probably be expanded to include other cultigens suited to non-alluvial soils of the region. [Hudson 1974, p. 2]

Many swidden farmers began to adopt a more commercial orientation with the smallholding cultivation[3] of rubber from the 1900s onward since rubber can be maintained with minimal care and needs to be tapped only when the market is favored by relatively high export prices. Today the predominant pattern of agriculture in Indonesia is a mixture of swiddens and cash cropping, and most of the country's export crops are cultivated on a smallholder basis.

The utility of swidden agriculture in the outer islands, which has been the subject of much recent debate (Dove 1986), contrasts sharply with the intensive double- and multiple-cropping patterns associated with small farm wet rice culture in Java. The typical Javanese farmer operates within the narrow confines of having access to only very small plots and must put the soil into continuous service with a cropping pattern that varies according to whether the land is irrigated (*sawah*) wet rice or unirrigated dry land (*tegalan*). Many farmers will have both kinds of land under cultivation in addition to a house garden in which they grow fruits and vegetables. Approximately 50 percent of all smallholder cultivated land in Java is *sawah* land, with 50 percent being mostly unirrigated land along with coastal ponds (Birowo and Hansen 1981, p. 3).

Of the *sawah* land in Java, more than 40 percent has modern irrigation facilities, enabling farmers to plant rice crops in both the wet and dry seasons. The remaining *sawah* land is dependent on more elementary rain-fed systems that frequently allow for only a wet season rice crop, followed by the planting of soybeans, maize, or other secondary crops in the dry season. Corn, cassava, soybeans, groundnuts, and sweet potatoes are the dominant crop selections in dry, or *tegalan*, areas.

The overall picture of agriculture land use in Indonesia shows considerable variation from the intensive use in the small, heavily populated islands of Java and Bali where 47 percent of the total land area is under cultivation to a markedly lower land use in the outer islands areas.[4] Thus, the land area under cultivation for agricultural purposes in Sumatra averages only 11 percent of the total land area, while in Sulawesi and Kalimantan it is even lower: 9 percent and 3.1 percent respectively

**Table 1.3.**
**Land Use in Indonesia**

| Region | Total Area | Agricultural Land Farms | Agricultural Land Estates | Forested Land | Denuded Land | Other Land |
|---|---|---|---|---|---|---|
| | | **Absolute Values** (*thousands of hectares*) | | | | |
| Sumatra | 47,361 | 3,803 | 1,314 | 24,735 | 4,757 | 12,752 |
| Java and Madura | 13,219 | 5,505 | 678 | 2,698 | 494 | 3,844 |
| Bali and Nusa Tenggara | 7,361 | 1,209 | 16 | 1,524 | 1,092 | 3,520 |
| Kalimantan | 53,946 | 1,868 | 59 | 39,774 | 2,486 | 9,659 |
| Sulawesi | 18,922 | 1,524 | 128 | 7,565 | 3,364 | 6,341 |
| Maluku | 7,450 | 260 | 30 | 5,872 | 214 | 1,074 |
| Irian Jaya | 42,198 | — | — | 31,500 | 154 | 10,544[a] |
| Total | 190,457 | 14,168 | 2,226 | 113,668 | 12,661 | 47,734[a] |
| | | **Relative Contribution** (*percent*) | | | | |
| Sumatra | 100 | 8 | 3 | 52 | 10 | 27 |
| Java and Madura | 100 | 42 | 5 | 20 | 4 | 29 |
| Bali and Nusa Tenggara | 100 | 16 | 0.2 | 21 | 15 | 48 |
| Kalimantan | 100 | 3 | 0.1 | 74 | 5 | 18 |
| Sulawesi | 100 | 8 | 1 | 40 | 18 | 33 |
| Maluku | 100 | 4 | 0.4 | 79 | 3 | 14 |
| Irian Jaya | 100 | — | — | 75 | 0.4 | 25[a] |
| Total % of Land | 100 | 7 | 1 | 60 | 7 | 25[a] |

*Source:* Indonesia, Bureau of Statistics (1973, 1975).

*Note:* No data for East Timur are included.

[a] Agricultural land of Irian Jaya is included as other land due to lack of data.

(Table 1.3). Only 8 percent of the total land area of Indonesia is currently being used for agriculture, and 60 percent is covered by forest. As noted earlier (see Table 1.2), however, the estimates of areas of potential agriculture use are greater.

The most important crops in Indonesia are rice, cassava, corn, sweet potatoes, sugar, coconut, peanut, and the estate crops of rubber, palm oil, soybeans, coffee, palm, tea, cloves, pepper, and tobacco. Of the other agricultural products, timber, both uncultivated and sawn, is the most valuable (Table 1.4). Rice is the major crop on Java where, under the intensive systems of cultivation supported by extensive irrigation systems, two or three crops can be obtained a year. Rice production since the mid 1970s has begun to expand to the outer islands as a result of the large government programs supporting rice production and the movement of people—particularly from Java and Bali—under the national transmigration program to the outer islands areas, who transfer in this process their intensive rice production practices. Java also

**Table 1.4.**
**Major Agricultural Products 1981/1982–1982/1983**
(*thousands of tons*)

| No. | Items | 1981/1982 | 1982/1983 |
|---|---|---|---|
| 1. | Rice | 22,288 | 23,191 |
| 2. | Uncultivated timber | 15,376 | 13,015 |
| 3. | Cassava | 13,648 | 12,676 |
| 4. | Corn | 4,648 | 3,207 |
| 5. | Sawn timber | 2,500 | 6,046 |
| 6. | Sweet Potatoes | 2,034 | 1,897 |
| 7. | Sugar | 1,913 | 1,862 |
| 8. | Coconut/copra | 1,812 | 1,736 |
| 9. | Rubber | 1,046 | 861 |
| 10. | Palm-oil | 748 | 873 |
| 11. | Soybeans | 687 | 514 |
| 12. | Peanuts | 505 | 434 |
| 13. | Coffee | 295 | 265 |
| 14. | Palm | 135 | 147 |
| 15. | Tobacco | 118 | 117 |
| 16. | Tea | 109 | 92 |
| 17. | Pepper | 39 | 37 |
| 18. | Cloves | 40.2 | 31 |
| 19. | Cotton | 10 | 18 |

*Source:* Indonesia, Department of Information (1984).

accounts for 75 percent of the country's total corn production, 60 percent of its sweet potatoes, 80 percent of its cassava, 90 percent of its soybeans, and 100 percent of its sugar output. The outer islands, in contrast, provide the majority of the country's timber and plantation crops (Birowo and Hansen 1981, p. 3).

Looking at the overall use of land in Indonesia, one is struck by five major features. The first is the importance of agriculture, being the most predominant economic activity. Agriculture engages 57 percent of the total labor force. The agriculture sector in the early 1980s accounted for the largest share (24 percent), even dwarfing oil (18 percent), of the country's gross national product, was the second major export earner, and provided some 20 percent of the government's tax revenue (World Bank 1985, p. 94).[5]

The second feature is the existence of two very distinct types of cultivation: the intensive form of cultivation found on Java and Bali and, in marked contrast, the extensive swidden type found in the far larger areas of the outer islands.

The third feature is the prominence of smallholder production, whether in plantation crops, in rice, or in other secondary food crops. Even though the commercial plantations are an important feature of Indonesia's agriculture sector, particularly in the outer islands areas, smallholder production remains the dominant organizational mode of production, producing two-thirds of the total rubber, nearly all the copra and coffee, and all rice and other secondary food crops. On Java approximately 5.4 million hectares are under smallholder cultivation in contrast to 67,600 hectares under estate control; in Sumatra, the figure is 3.8 million hectares as against 1.3 million hectares under estates; and in Sulawesi and Kalimantan, the plantation sector accounts for less then 10 percent of total land under cultivation. Overall smallholder farmers occupy about 87 percent of the agricultural land and the estates, only 13 percent (Birowo and Hansen 1981, p. 4).

The fourth feature is the lack, in contrast to many countries, of large landholdings. Indonesia does not suffer from a high degree of tenancy: 74.8 percent of all farms are owner operated, and only 65,466 farms, or 0.5 percent from the national total of 14 million, are of 10 hectares or more in size. These larger farms are almost entirely on the outer islands where both tree crops and shifting cultivation leads to larger farm sizes. In contrast, Java has a notable predominance of small farms of 0.5 hectare and less (Indonesia, Bureau of Statistics 1984). Overall, 71 percent of the farms throughout Indonesia are fewer than 1 hectare in size (Table 1.5).

**Table 1.5.**
**Distribution of Farm Holdings, by Size, 1973**
(*percent*)

| Region | Less than 0.5 Hectare | 0.5–1 Hectare | 1–5 Hectares | 5 and More Hectares |
|---|---|---|---|---|
| Java | 57 | 25 | 17 | 1 |
| Sumatra | 29 | 26 | 42 | 3 |
| Kalimantan | 22 | 21 | 43 | 14 |
| Sulawesi | 25 | 24 | 47 | 3 |
| Other Islands | 31 | 23 | 42 | 4 |
| Indonesia | 46 | 25 | 27 | 2 |

*Source:* Indonesia, Bureau of Statistics (1973).

The fifth feature is the importance of the agriculture sector and of agricultural policy and planning in Indonesia. Still a predominantly agricultural country, in 1980 78 percent of Indonesia's population was living in rural areas. With a population increase of some 3 percent a year, it has faced and will face problems of food shortages and of growing rural underemployment that will require effective government policy intervention. One striking aspect of the New Order government's ability to deal with these problems is the achievement by the early 1980s of self-sufficiency in rice production as a result of a number of major government programs. These programs can be traced back to the Kasimo plan of the early the 1950s aimed at increasing rice production, to the campaigns and loans of the late 1950s, and to the widespread BIMAS rice intensification program of the 1970s, all of which reflect the constant struggle to increase rice production. Increasing production has been a difficult task because of the political uncertainties of postindependence times, particularly in the 1950s and 1960s, with the added hazards of major plagues or unduly long dry seasons that have affected crops in different years. It was not until the early 1980s that the country was at last achieving what appears to be full self-sufficiency in rice.

Throughout these periods the agriculture sector was given primary investment priority in government national development plans, reflecting the fact that in the 1970s 66 percent of all employed persons were in the agriculture sector. While this figure had decreased to 57 percent in 1980 (World Bank 1985, p. 94), the increase in agriculture incomes and the ability of the agriculture sector, particularly in the outer islands, to absorb the expected growth in the labor force in the next few decades underline the continuing importance of the agriculture sector and, with it, of agricultural policy in Indonesia. At the beginning of the 1980s, agriculture in the outer islands accounted for over two-thirds of the total employment and three-quarters of rural employment and was the largest single source of new employment. Not surprisingly, the 1983 state guidelines for national policy (GBHN) emphasized the importance of Indonesian agriculture development:

> [A]gricultural development in a broader sense, needs continuous improvement with the aim to boost agricultural production so as to meet the need for food and the requirements of domestic industries, but also to step up exports, increase the earnings of farmers, expand employment opportunities, encourage equitable business opportunities, support regional development and to intensify transmigration activities. [GBHN 1983, Chapter 4]

## Social and Political Importance of Land

One is immediately struck by a number of aspects of the social and political importance of land in Indonesia. One is the widely different systems of land rights that exist throughout the country that to the present have not been fully rationalized. Historically, two types of land systems existed in Indonesia before a unified system was introduced with the Basic Agrarian Law (BAL) of 1960. One type was that of the traditional *adat* rights, which still exists in many parts of Indonesia, where land is owned and handed down according to *adat* law without formal registration or title. A second is the more Westernized system of written land titles and land registration introduced under the Dutch in the colonial era and that has remained, although limited mainly to urban areas. The present national land system introduced with the BAL of 1960 provides a comprehensive legal system covering both types of land rights. This system has not, however, been fully implemented, and consequently, landownership and land rights in Indonesia are still not fully formalized although the area is becoming of increasing importance with rapid development in both urban and rural areas in the last two decades.

One striking aspect of landownership and land use in Indonesia is the pattern in the small, although important, central island of Java where the very high population densities combined with limited land and thus small landholdings create a very narrow line between subsistence and poverty in contrast to other parts of the country. Even if the average farm holding in Java is small but still adequate, many of the landowners frequently lose their ownership. One reason for such loss is smallholders' indebtedness to moneylenders. The small farmers consequently become sharecroppers who cultivate their land only to hand over a sizable portion of the harvest to creditors. At the same time the traditional *bengkok* system of land, which involves the allocation of what is often the better village land to village officials, leaves the majority of villagers with the less cultivable land. Owing to the high population pressure and the unavailability of new land in Java, access there to additional agricultural land is also very limited.

These problems in landownership and land fragmentation are accentuated by inheritance practices that in turn lead to the large-scale involvement in off-farm activities and what has been observed by one author as occupational multiplicity as a survival strategy for many of the poor households on Java (Jones 1981). One of the great attractions of the large and often controversial Indonesian transmigration program that moves peasant farmers from Java to the outer islands where living conditions are usually far from attractive is the fact that each family receives 2 hectares of land for cultivation and thus access to land that is denied them in Java.

Land plays an important political part in Indonesian life although in a different way from many countries that face the more common problems of large landowners. Land, land problems, and land conflicts in Indonesia have historically often proved to be sources of major agrarian discontent (Kartodirdjo 1973). In more modern days land and land-associated problems have not emerged as strongly as major political rallying points except in the context of the pressure to change the colonial system. The BAL, which has not been particularly successful, resulted in the introduction of the BAL of 1960. Although the failure of the BAL in itself has not caused undue dissatisfaction, land problems have served as a rallying point of more general discontent. In what is a strikingly controlled society in political terms under the New Order, land problems provide one of the few means of acceptable open public discontent, and dissatisfaction over land issues has led on a number of occasions to demonstrations and complaints to the country's National Assembly in Jakarta over land rights issues in both rural and urban areas.

## Notes

1. In spite of a long tradition of soil investigations, the depth of current knowledge about Indonesian soils is extremely variable and is inadequate for even the broadest

type of land-use planning over many areas. This inadequacy is explained largely by the tremendous area of the country and the difficulty of carrying out investigations in the densely forested, sparsely inhabited regions. In terms of land use no breakdown of overall land use based on up-to-date surveys is available.

2. See Indonesia, Bureau of Statistics (1984, p. 46). In 1980 61.9 percent of Indonesian total population lived on Java and Madura, 20 percent in Sumatra, 7 percent in Sulawesi, 4.6 percent in Kalimantan, and the balance lived in the other islands.

3. Smallholding is a term used in reference to single-farmer cultivation of small areas of land, usually below two hectares.

4. Figures for both potential agriculture land use and land under cultivation vary from source to source due to lack of data on certain areas—notably, Timor Timur and Irian Jaya. Thus, in this calculation, agriculture land use for neither Irian Jaya nor Timor Timur is included.

5. While agriculture remains the predominant economic activity, there are wide variations in the number of people engaged in agriculture in Java and on the outer islands. Java has a much more varied employment structure than the outer islands, with only 51 percent working in agriculture in 1980 and a far higher percentage working in manufacturing, trade, and services. In contrast, 68 percent of the workers in the outer islands in 1980 worked in the agriculture sector and a far lower percentage in trade (8 percent), manufacturing (6 percent), and services (6 percent). See World Bank (1985, p. 96, Table 4.2).

# 2

---

# Land Policy in Indonesia

## *The Colonial Period*

The initial steps toward evolving a specific policy to deal with land problems in Indonesia were taken in the period of colonial rule from the seventeenth century to 1947. Thus, the consolidation of the East India Company's power in the seventeenth century saw the first step with the introduction of a system of compulsory levies from the local rulers to the foreign power that indirectly caused considerable hardship to the individual cultivators, often leaving them with only the barest means of subsistence (Furnivall 1944; Day 1966). Pressure for changes in this system grew in the eighteenth century, but nothing new was attempted until the arrival of Raffles in the early years of the nineteenth century who, with his previous experience with land affairs in India—particularly in Madras—took the first steps toward reforming the system. Raffles initially set up the McKenzie Commission in 1811 to examine the background of agrarian problems and to recommend to the colonial government the best way to maximize the use of land. Finding that all land in Indonesia at that time was owned either by the government or by the rajas, the commission determined that the land could be taxed for the benefit of the colonial government. This led to the introduction by Raffles of a tax of two-fifths of the farmer's product, a tax that remained in effect most of the nineteenth century.

Throughout the colonial period the government was committed to making the colony pay and relied largely on the productive powers of the Javanese peasantry to do this. In this they followed the practice of the Javanese rulers of earlier times, but unlike those rulers, the colonial government was not merely concerned with drawing off a proportion of the rice grown by its subjects but also with producing and delivering a wide range of export crops with a good deal more regularity and accountability. There was also a constant colonial demand for more peasant labor, reflected in the many references to the labor question (*arbeidvraagstuk*) in nineteenth century official documents.

The main island of Java was in generally poor condition. Raffles noted that "over far the greater part, seven eights [*sic*] of the island, the soil is either neglected or badly cultivated and the population scanty. It is by the produce of the remaining eighth that the whole nation is supported" (1817, p. 108). But he also saw Java's potential, noting that "many of the best spots still remain uncultivated and several districts are almost deserts and neglected which might be the seats of the crowded and happy peasantry" (p. 69). Both in the reforms he carried out and in his perceptions of the problems to be faced, Raffles was a major figure in shaping Indonesian land policy in this early period. Unfortunately, there was a major weakness in the system he sought to establish. From his Indian experience Raffles based his system on the need for a detailed land cadastre (or register) and expected to get the necessary land data for this from the village chiefs. In practice, however, the chiefs had no accurate data and met the demand for it by frequently handing in inaccurate or fictitious data, with the result that Raffles's new system proved in the end to be as inequitable as the old one.

With the return of the Dutch, the colonial organization of peasant labor after 1830 was organized under the so-called cultivation system. Under this system the cultivators, instead of paying a land rent or tax, paid their dues to the government by devoting a percentage of their land, usually one-fifth, and time to growing an export crop. Apart from growing this crop they had other duties. They had to provide compulsory labor service including compulsory labor for active officials, compulsory labor on public works, and labor to fill the village's needs. This system unfortunately led to excessive demands on the peasants' time, leaving them little time to grow the rice crop vital to their own subsistence, and in some areas serious famines, such as the Cirebon famine in the early 1840s, ensued.

This system broke up the large land holdings that had existed previously into smaller parcels as the enormous demands for labor necessitated the spreading of the burden of the labor service (Kumar 1980, p. 586). This breakup was done by reclassifying land that hitherto had been hereditary to individual families into communal or village land so that it would be divided among a greater number of people. A further important result of this system and of the demand for greater efficiency in general under colonial rule in the nineteenth century was the gradual shaping of the Javanese village into a better defined entity than it had been before. Boundaries were now more sharply drawn; regulations that required official sanction for the amalgamation of villages were enacted; and the position of the village head became more formalized. While the village head was still elected, his position was more fully utilized by higher levels of government. The increased responsibility that ensued from the greater recognition of his position in turn enhanced his authority and also his advantageous position in the village, particularly in relation to owning land.

Large landholdings still existed, however, in two forms. One of these was the so-called private lands that at some time had been alienated by the colonial government to private individuals. These estates were to remain essentially intact until the end of the colonial period. Second, there existed a particular type of village, the *pendidikan desa*, that had a special legal status that exempted it from taxation and service because of its religious function. Although these were of a limited number, with only about 150 in Java in 1912, the heads of these villages were appointed by the district head and often had exceptionally large landholdings.

The end of the century, what has been termed the *liberal period* (1870–1900), saw the phasing out of the cultivation system in favor of private entrepreneurs moving into the Indies. After 1870 they were permitted to rent peasant land on an almost unlimited scale. At the same time land was becoming less plentiful on Java. Some districts in Central Java had virtually no more land available for *sawah* as early as 1831 although, in contrast, in other areas such as some in West Java the fragmentation of landholdings only occurred toward the turn of the century. It would seem that those who held land became entrenched in their holdings in any particular village as land became scarcer.

One saw in the colonial period two distinct legal systems of land laws. One system existed for non-Indonesians and foreigners, and a second system was for Indonesians. Citizenship essentially determined which system of land law would govern landownership and control. For non-Indonesians and Western Europeans, a civil law system prevailed in which lands were surveyed, registered, and titled based on Western civil law procedures. For Indonesians *adat*, or customary law, was followed and holdings were not surveyed, registered, or titled.

## Postindependence: The Pre-Reform Years (1947–1960)

The early period of Indonesia's independence, from 1947 to the enactment of the BAL of 1960, was characterized by the dual system of land laws that was carried over from colonial times. Citizenship essentially determined which system of land law would govern land ownership and control. For non-Indonesians, lands continued as in colonial times to be surveyed, registered, and titled based on Western civil law procedures. For Indonesians, common or customary law (*adat*) was followed, with landholdings usually being unsurveyed, unregistered, and nontitled. Landownership and landholdings under *adat* were based on community acceptance of recognized land boundaries, oral and written documents attesting to ownership, and claims by individuals and groups. There were minimal written documents under the *adat* system and thus a lack of evidence to prove landownership or title. In contrast, lands titled under Western law procedures were usually cadastrally surveyed with documentation and legal descriptions, specific written documentation with registration documentation, number and control documents, and written evidence of title for specific owners and land parcels. Under the dual system, which prevailed from colonial times to 1960, it is estimated that less than 5 percent of all land in Indonesia was titled under the Western titling system, leaving more than 95 percent of the land in the country untitled yet recognized under *adat* ownership and control. In addition, with the virtual lack of titling in the country, it was not possible to determine the amount of land that was not under some type of ownership claim and thereby could be considered unfettered Indonesia *tanah negara*, or state land.

The period immediately following independence in Indonesia was one of reform and transition. It was reform in the sense of a newly independent nation attempting to rectify a system of law that was seen as exploitive in nature and penalizing to native Indonesians. It was transitive in the sense it was trying to evolve a new land law system that would eliminate the dualistic system. Consequently, activities during this period were directed to two major areas of concern. The first was that of land tenure, with efforts being directed to resolving matters of land reform, land redistribution, illegal settlements, sharecropping arrangements, the breakup of estates, landlord-tenant relationships, and other types of tenant-user-related activities. The second concern was that of land law itself, and thus concurrently with the activities in land tenure matters, efforts were also initiated to revise the agrarian law system. Directly after independence in 1947, several state commissions were created to develop a new land law for the country. In such a sensitive area as land law, there were divergent viewpoints in the country as to what type of law would be appropriate for the newly independent nation.

During the lengthy discussion period that ensued in the years after independence, it became evident that there were two major and opposite views. One group favored a total overhaul in the land law system with the

major emphasis on land reform, land redistribution, and the appropriation of large landholdings. The second group favored a continuation
of the previously existing system and related tenure arrangements. Of
those in the first group, there was also a split between those who favored
a continuation of the dual system (i.e., Western civil and *adat*) and those
who felt that the law should be a totally *adat* system. Protracted debates
and discussions ensued, resulting finally in a compromise law, the BAL
of 1960.

## The Basic Agrarian Law of 1960

The BAL, enacted September 24, 1960, retains certain elements of the
previously existing land law system while also providing a new approach
that was appropriate to the Indonesians' changed situation and requirements. Since it is the foundation of modern land law, administration,
and policy in Indonesia, it is examined in detail.

The BAL, or *Undang-Undang Pokok Agraria*, is based on Article 33 of
the 1945 Constitution of the Republic of Indonesia and Principle 5 of
the state philosophy of *Pancasila*. Article 33 of the constitution specifies
that land in Indonesia has a social function and that all land matters
are controlled by the State of Indonesia as the representative authority
of the people of Indonesia. Principle 5 of the *Pancasila* specifies that to
provide a just and prosperous society, adequate supplies of food and
clothing must be provided for the populace. Land in this context is seen
as the fundamental provider of food and clothing. This view, it should
be noted, is in direct contrast to the Western concept of land as an
economic or commercial commodity to be bought and sold in a market
economy with financial return as the main consideration.

The philosophical base on which the BAL rested had been laid out
in two other government statements by President Soekarnos prior to
the enactment of the BAL. These statements included President Soekarnos' well-known *Political Manifesto* address on August 17, 1959 and his
address to the first session of the People's Advisory Council (D.P.R.) on
January 13, 1960 (Utrecht 1969, p. 71–2). Both emphasized the unique
and all-important role of land in Indonesia and the need for the formulation of a comprehensive land law that reflected the country's predominantly agrarian nature.

The BAL consists of sixty-seven articles divided into four chapters
covering basic principles and provisions; rights of land, water, and space;
as well as land registration, penal provisions, and transitional provisions.
The law revises the former agrarian law of Indonesia as it existed in

1960 and promulgates a new comprehensive approach to all land law and land-use-related matters in the country.

The basic principles that provide the framework for the detailed legislation include the following:

*Foundation of the Law:* The entire earth, water, air, and natural resources of Indonesia are gifts of God Almighty and constitute the wealth of the nation (Article 1).

*Control and Authority:* The state, on behalf of the whole people of Indonesia, is responsible for the control and regulation of earth, water, air, and natural resources of the nation to achieve the maximum prosperity of the people in terms of happiness, welfare, and freedom in the society. Such authority may be delegated to appropriate specified governmental entities (Article 2).

*Adat Community Lands: Adat* property rights shall be adjusted to the national law and interests and shall not be in conflict with such national laws and regulations (Article 3).

*Rights Authorized:* Several types of land rights, under the state's direction and control, may be granted to and owned by persons and corporations (Article 4).

*Adat: Adat* applies to agrarian matters unless it conflicts with national and state interests, Indonesian socialism, and legislative regulations, in which case the national law provisions prevail (Article 5).

*Function of Land Rights:* All land rights have a social function (Article 6).

*Land Ownership and Control:* Excessive ownership and control of land is not permitted (Article 7).

*State Regulation of Natural Resource Exploitation:* All exploitation of natural resources shall be regulated by the state (Article 8).

*Rights of Indonesian Citizens:* Only Indonesian Citizens, regardless of being male or female, may have the fullest use of the earth, water, and air resources of the nation (Article 9).

*Agricultural Land:* Persons and corporations with land rights for agricultural purposes are obliged to cultivate or exploit the land by themselves and not to use extortionate methods (Article 10).

*Legal Relationships with the Society:* Legal relationships between persons and corporations with the land and resources are to be regulated to achieve maximum prosperity for the people while preventing excessive control over the livelihood of other persons. The different needs, both economic and legal, of society shall be considered, including the need to ensure the protection of economically weak groups (Article 11).

*Mutual Assistance and Interests:* All agrarian efforts, regardless of whether by state or other parties, shall be based on the principle of *gotong royong* (working together) (Article 12).

*Standard of Living:* All agrarian undertakings shall be regulated to increase production, to increase the people's prosperity, and to guarantee Indonesian citizens a standard of living suitable to human dignity. Private monopolies shall be prevented and state activities of a monopolistic nature may be carried out only by special act. Social guarantees and security are to be promoted by the government (Article 13).

*Natural Resources Plan:* A general plan providing for the reservation, appropriation, and use of the earth, water, air, and natural resources shall be prepared to provide for the needs of the state; religious and sacred needs; needs for economic, social, cultural, and welfare purposes; needs for agricultural production, cattle breeding, and fisheries; and needs for industry, transmigration, and mining. Regional governments are responsible for regulation of such resource uses in their respective regions (Article 14).

*Conservation Requirement:* Land cultivation must prevent damage to the land resource as well as improve the fertility of the soil (Article 15).

*Description of Rights:* The various types of rights on land, water, and in air space are stipulated (Article 16).

*Size of Holdings:* Both the maximum and/or minimum size of land that may be owned and controlled by an individual or corporation will be regulated. Land areas held in excess of the maximum are to be redistributed to the people based on need. Compensation to owners whose lands are taken shall be made. Attainment of the minimum area limit is established as a goal to be accomplished over time on a gradual basis (Article 17).

*Annulment of Rights:* Where it is to the benefit of the public interest, lands owned under any type of land right may be acquired by the government with compensation to be made to the owner (Article 18).

With these principles the BAL introduced a system of control and regulation over virtually all aspects of land and land-use activities in Indonesia. It also marked two notable changes in previous land regulation and practice. First, it revoked all the old land registration and titling laws and regulations. This revocation essentially eliminated the dual (i.e., Western and *adat*) system of land law and in lieu provided for an entirely new system of unique Indonesian applicability. Lands previously titled under the provisions of Western law could be converted to the new system, but failure to do this would lead to forfeiture, with the land reverting to state ownership. Second, it established an entirely new law that would have its own implementation regulations. Of key significance in the new law was the establishment of a system of land rights with varying degrees of tenure and with different citizenship requirements determining the type of right to be granted. Of equal significance was the proviso that in all land law matters the BAL would govern and take precedence over the *adat* system of land law. Rights acquired, however, under *adat* prior to enactment of BAL were fully protected, and such lands could be registered and titled under the new system.

The law also laid out clearly two important elements: those of the limits of the size (both maximum and minimum) of landownership and of the priorities in distribution. In terms of landholdings the maximum limit of land area in sparsely populated areas (under 50 people per square kilometer) was set at 15 hectares for rice fields (*sawah*) or 20 hectares for dry land (*tanah kering*). In densely populated areas (over 401 people per square kilometer), the maximum size was 5 hectares for rice fields or 6 hectares for dry land. In no situation could the combined area be over 20 hectares. The BAL also established a minimum limit of ownership of agricultural land of 2 hectares for either rice fields or dry land. The primary goal here was to prevent the further division of agricultural land. In addition, the BAL stipulated that a landowner could not control, through ownership, land pledge, or lease, agricultural land outside the subdistrict or adjoining subdistrict in which he or she controls more than 2 hectares.[1]

As to distribution of land, priority was given to peasants who were cultivating the land in question and the regular peasant workers of the ex-owners, with special priority being given to veterans and widows of former independence fighters. The beneficiaries were given 16 years to pay the government the price to be reimbursed to the former owner for the distributed land. Landowners who rejected or boycotted the takeover by the government of their excess land for distribution to peasants would be punished by 3 months' detention and no compensation for the land.

## Land Registration

The BAL required (Article 19) that all land be registered, a feature that provided legal security to landowners. Land registration was to include the measuring, surveying, and mapping of land; the registration of land rights; and the issuance of certificates of land rights. How this was to be done in practice was laid out in a series of implementation regulations issued by the Department of Home Affairs. Regulations providing for registration requirements and procedures were promulgated and issued as Act No. 10 of 1961, effective March 23, 1961. Registration was to serve as evidence of the legal validity of land transfer actions for sale and purchase (*jual/beli*), gift (*hadiah*), auction (*lelang*), exchange (*tukar*), inheritance (*pembagian harta warisan*), annulment and cancellation of rights (*ganti rugi*), and encumbrances (*crediet verband* and *hipotik*). Another key aspect of registration was the establishment of what types of rights could be held by specific classes of individuals and corporations (Indonesians, foreigners, and Indonesian or foreign corporations). Thus, registration was aimed at establishing and delineating which lands were privately owned and which lands were stateowned (*tanah negara*) and establishing a cadastre of private and state-owned lands.

**Mapping and Surveying Procedures.** A map is required under the BAL [Part II, Article 19, Sections (1) and (2)] as a requirement of the measuring, mapping, and recording of lands. The Cadastral Survey System in Indonesia in the early 1980s had reached the point at which a series of individual village base maps, or plats, were prepared from ground surveys and in some cases aerial photography. In addition, a national geodetic control was started in 1974, using a new set of geoid parameters that provided a more precise positioning of points into the UTM (Universal Transverse Mercator) system. A first-order control network was established throughout the major Indonesian islands with the exception of portions of Sumatra. These first-order control/triangulation stations were 30 to 60 kilometers apart, and positions were determined by Doppler observations to geodetic satellites. Precision in this system is claimed to be 1 part in 250,000 for independent station observations and a relative precision between stations of 1 part in 100,000. Full completion of the net at 30 to 60 kilometer distance between stations is expected in the mid 1980s (USAID 1982, p. 18).

In 1982/1983 the densification of this program was initiated to reduce the distance between first-order geodetic triangulation stations to between 15 and 17 kilometers. The prime purpose for this densification was to produce 1:25,000 scale national maps, but it would also provide a better net to tie the local coordinate system control into the national net. The first areas of densification were in East Java and Bali with later extensions to Central and West Java and parts of Sumatra. It is also planned that at least one first-order station would be established in the larger urban areas with populations of 100,000 or more.

The establishment of this system fits in with the role of mapping as part of any land registration procedure. The basic directives for establishing this system were laid down in a regulation of the Minister of Agrarian Affairs, Regulation No. 6 of 1961 (Articles 1 and 31). Before areas can be selected as land registration areas, they must have basic ground control established that will be used later as a control net for position reference. This basic ground control can be established by terrestrial and/or photogrammetric methods and, in terms of efficiency, could be established for one village or for a number of villages.

An examination of the cadastral survey process as it is applied in Indonesia highlights a number of procedures for different types of measurements:

*Individual parcel:* If application for a letter of measurement is made for a parcel where no previous measurement has been made or for a parcel that has been subdivided into two or more new parcels, then the Directorate for Land Registration (DPT) would make an individual measurement for those parcels by the terrestrial method.

*Complete village measurement:* The DPT can by regulation complete the measurement of all parcels in a village without requiring applications for a letter of measurement by the entire village either by the terrestrial or the photogrammetric methods.

*Multiple village measurement:* As in the complete village procedure, multiple villages can be measured under a large area program. In this situation the photogrammetric method is used.

*Transmigration areas:* In transmigration areas the parcels are predetermined on detailed site plans prepared by the Department of Public Works and then laid out on the ground by DPT terrestrial crews.

Looking at these procedures in more detail, an application for a letter of measurement (*surat ukur*) is made by the applicant for a land title by initially submitting an application form (*Surat Pernyataan*). Once this application is made to the district office, the parcel is measured and depicted on the letter of measurement. A copy is placed in the *Buku Tanah*, and the original is placed in the Register of Letters of Measurement. A copy of the *Buku Tanah*, which includes the letter of measurement, is given to the titleholder. The cadastral survey is then carried out. This survey is made by a number of terrestrial and photogrammetric procedures, depending on the terrain. Where aerial photography is possible over relatively flat areas, the photogrammetric method is used, and where the terrain is steep and for other areas for which photography would be difficult, the terrestrial method is used (see Appendix A for a discussion of these procedures, their advantages and disadvantages, and details of a special procedure used for transmigration areas).

**Registration of Land Rights.** Under the BAL two types of land are defined: privately owned land and state-owned land (*tanah negara*). Unless land is held under a valid claim of title, the presumption is that the land is state land. Private land can thus be either land held under *adat* with no title issued or land that has been titled. If it is titled land, then it may be land titled under the BAL or land for which formerly a civil law or Western title had been issued. State land can be either titled or untitled land, but with the BAL it now had to be titled. If the land is under *adat* while the BAL (Articles 3 and 5) sanctions *adat*, it also requires that *adat* be adjusted where it is in conflict with the provisions of the BAL and that in cases of conflict the BAL governs.

Article 16 of the BAL specifies the following various types of authorized rights:

Right of ownership (*hak milik*),

Right of exploitation (*hak guna usaha*),

Right of building (*hak bangunan*),

Right of use (*hak pakai*),

Right of opening up land (*hak membuka tanah*),

Right of collecting forest products (*hak memungut hasil hutan*).

The type of security or tenure of these rights ranges from full legal ownership (*hak milik*), to long-term lease (*hak guna usaha*), and to short-term temporary permit (*hak membuka tanah* and *hak memungut hasil hutan*). Only Indonesian citizens and Indonesian corporations, subject to certain exceptions, may hold rights of ownership. Certain rights of a temporary nature (e.g., land pledge, *hak gadai*; sharecrop, *hak bagi hasil*; or lodging, *hak menempati*) can also be regulated under the provisions of the BAL.

The BAL contains provisions that regulate the various steps in the registration process. These include the original or initial registration and certification; any transfer (sales, gift, auction, exchange, inheritance); and any encumbrances (*hipotik, crediet verband*). Original registration includes titling of both *adat* and state land. Provisions are made for the replacement of certificates that have been lost, destroyed, or damaged.

Unfortunately in terms of the actual implementation of this new system, the BAL made it mandatory that land be registered but imposed no time limit within which registration had to be accomplished. It stated only that the responsibility of the government was to encourage and facilitate land registration activities in a timely manner. The BAL also did not provide full legal guarantee of ownership through registration since it laid down that the issuance of certificates of rights on land is only strong (but not final) evidence of ownership (BAL, Article 19). This point, as we will see later, was a major weakness in the legislation that was seriously to affect the implementation of the new system.

Two approaches were formulated in subsequent years for land registration under the BAL. One became known as the *sporadic* method where the government responded to applications for registration on a case-by-case basis. Other than responding to applications filed, the government made no attempt to influence the volume of registration with this approach. This system is basically applicant based, making it, in effect, a passive program. The second was the *systematic* method where a massive effort was made by the government to effect registrations on a large scale. This effort involved the government's aggressive promotion of a registration program by outreach programs, public information, mass surveys, mass production of certificates, and other techniques designed to produce a high volume of issued certificates. This much more aggressive and action-oriented program allowed the government to control registration.

In practice, the sporadic approach was to become the most common approach. This, unfortunately, was not to prove satisfactory because of the large number of land titles in Indonesia that needed processing, the small amount of land already registered in 1960, the small size and number of parcels of land, and the long delays in the registration process. In addition, the costs of registration in most cases had to be borne by the applicant, which tended to limit registration.

*Registration Procedures.* The authority for registration as provided under the BAL is as follows: Under Articles 2, 4, and 19, the Government of Indonesia is responsible for land registration, with functional responsibility being delegated to the Department of Home Affairs and operationally assigned within the ministry to the Directorate Generals of Agrarian Affairs.[2] Under this director general, a unit entitled the Directorate for Land Registration (*Pendaftaran Tanah*, DPT) has the responsibility for administration of the land registration requirements of the BAL (Figure 2.1). In addition, the Directorate General of Agrarian Affairs has offices in each province, city (Kotamadya), and district (Kabupaten), except for those areas where the population or settlement is too sparse to warrant maintenance of an office and where the provincial offices perform certain specified operations (Figure 2.2). In practice, the city and district offices are the key functional offices for purposes of land registration activities.

Land registration authority is delegated under BAL Articles 2 and 14 to the provinces with a provision that allows the delegation of authority to the *adat* communities, although in practice this has never been implemented. The Minister of Home Affairs Regulation No. 6 of

**Figure 2.1.** *Organization of Land Administration: Central Government.*

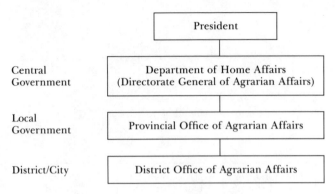

**Figure 2.2.** *Land Administration in Indonesia.*

1972 contains details of the full delegation of authority, together with limitations on which organizational levels may take specific actions.

*Types of Registration.* While the total registration process is commonly referred to as *land registration*, administratively the term *registration* in Indonesia normally refers to the mapping and measuring part of the process, and *titling* refers to the adjudication of rights and the issuance of title documents. The basic registration documentation established and maintained at the city and/or district levels consists of four registers:

Name list (*daftar nama*): This is a permanent file or list of individuals who own land in a given area. The list contains the owner's name and address, type of right, registration number, land area in hectares, and village (*desa*) location of the land.

Land list (*daftar tanah*): This contains a listing of the amount of land in a given area that is privately owned and that is state owned. Essentially this lists the ownership status of land by village and by city or district. The listing also contains information on rights of use such as road rights of way or powerline assessment.

Land book (*buku tanah*): This contains information on the types of rights registered and on the transfer of land. A separate book is maintained for each type of right on a parcel of land. Each land book that registers a title is also assigned a running number of the category of right and village location (e.g., Hak Milik, No. 321/Benteng).

Letter of measurement (*surat ukur*): This contains the areal measurement and boundary description of lands based on a survey and map. This registration serves as the basic legal evidence for the location, area, and boundaries of the lands involved. The boundary map establishes the extent of the land claimed under ownership by individuals. The map may be prepared from either a ground survey (terrestrial method) or aerial photograph (photogrammetric method). Regardless of which method is used, the map prepared constitutes legal sufficiency for purposes of land registration. For reference purposes each measurement certificate is assigned a running number according to the year it is issued (e.g., No. 123, 1982). The records (measurement and land book) are cross-referenced with the number designations.

**Types of Actions in Registration.** Registration, as specified under the BAL, is required for the following types of actions.

*Original issuance of title.* This includes initial registration and titling actions on lands that have not previously been titled. Lands included in these provisions are the following:

*Adat* lands: Lands held or claimed under customary law by individual or communities.

State lands: Land owned by the Republic of Indonesia without any outstanding claims and/or invalid claims. Certain state-owned lands may have had titles issued before, either under the BAL or Western title, that have since been annulled or canceled, and title has then reverted to the state.

Western titled lands: lands titled under Western or civil law procedures. Under the BAL such titles are to be converted to the title rights provided for by the BAL. Regardless of the type of title previously issued, these lands must be registered and titled under the provisions of the BAL.

The title claim for lands being held under *adat* may be based on one of two situations that hold regardless of whether an individual or community is asserting ownership:

Conversion: In this situation the claim of ownership predates the BAL and therefore originated prior to September 24, 1960. An individual may base the claim on a document issued to him or her or on evidence of purchase from prior owners/claimants. The term *conversion* denotes that the rights are converted from *adat* rights to rights under the provisions of the BAL.

Recognition: In this situation the claim of ownership originates after the BAL became effective on September 24, 1960. The claim is an *adat* right claim but one that postdates the effective date of the BAL. The claim is technically without legal validity because land unclaimed on September 24, 1960, was considered to be state-owned land (*tanah negara*), and the procedures for obtaining rights to such land were to be filed or obtained at that time under the BAL and the implementing regulations. However, for registration purposes, in practice the Indonesian government usually issues title to lands based on such types of claims unless there is a strong reason not to.

*Land Transfer.* Land transfer covers all the actions that result in a change of ownership from one owner to another. Transactions affecting ownership are required to be registered under the BAL (Article 19). The various types of rights in the BAL and their registration requirements are set forth in various sections (e.g., *hak milik*, Articles 20 and 23; *hak guna usaha*, Articles 28 and 32). Not all types of actions affecting ownership are required to be registered, particularly if they are temporary or of short-term duration. The major transfer actions that must be registered are as follows:

Sale of lands: This includes conveyances made without monetary consideration and gifts of land made in exchange for other gifts received.

Gift: This includes conveyances made without monetary consideration and gifts of land made in exchange for other gifts received.

Auction: This involves lands sold or auctioned off for default or foreclosure of security arrangements (*hipotik* and *crediet verband*).

Exchange: This involves exchanging land for other land, land for money, and land for a combination of land and money.

Inheritance: This involves the transfer of land owned by a deceased party. The transfer may be included in a will (testate) or by customary law (intestate).

*Registration of Encumbrances.* Encumbrances include actions where land is used as collateral or as security for obtaining funds. The BAL (Articles 25, 23, and 39) specifies the various land rights that may be used as security for debt and which security arrangements must be registered. The two major types of security arrangements are:

*Hipotik* (mortgage): The land is used as security for debt, and failure to pay the debt allows the creditors to sell the land to satisfy the amount due. Mortgages are registered in the records of the city and/or district Offices of Agrarian Affairs.

*Crediet verband* (security for credit arrangements): This involves obtaining credit on land subject to *adat* or customary law and to persons governed by *adat* law. Only certain types of Indonesian financial institutions may use this security arrangement. Procedurally, *crediet verband* security arrangements and *hipotik* are considered as security encumbrances on the land that can, upon certain conditions, result in the security holder obtaining title to the land or rights. Registration procedures for both *hipotik* and *crediet verband* are identical.

Under the provision of the BAL, both *hipotik* and *crediet verband* encumbrances are required to be registered. *Hipotik* may be effected on lands held under rights of *hak milik* (right of ownership), *hak guna bangunan* (right of building), and *hal guna usaha* (right of exploitation). *Crediet verband* may only be effected on lands subject to *adat* law. Registration requirements are essentially the same, and the same forms are used for both types of security arrangements.

Procedures for registration are as follows:

1. The individual seeking credit and the creditor execute a deed of *hipotik* or deed of security for credit before a land deed official (*notaris*) specifying the date of action, amount of credit, and duration of obligation.

2. The *hipotik* or *crediet verband* deeds, together with an application form and the required fees, are filed with the Office of Agraria at the city or district level for registration.

3. When the documentation is found to be in order, the Office of Agraria registers the *hipotik* or *crediet verband* right and issues documentation to that effect. The official land records in the Office of Agraria are noted, and copies of the registration date establishes the priority of the creditor in case of default. Registration is also required to remove from the records the notation of credit upon satisfaction of full payment or when damages are made in terms of the credit arrangements. Default on credit arrangements may result in a sale of the land used as security at public auction, while the funds obtained are used to repay the security holder.

**Procedures for Obtaining Titles.** The procedures for obtaining titles to land fall into two distinct processes, those referring to state-owned land and those referring to land under *adat*.

*State-Owned Land.* An applicant who wishes to use or obtain title to state-owned land must obtain the necessary application forms from an Office of Agrarian Affairs and complete the application with the required information. Depending on the type of right applied for, the application has to be filed in the appropriate office of agraria. For *hak milik* (right of ownership), *hak guna bangunan* (right of building), *hak pakai* (right of use), and *hak pengelolaan* (right of management), the application must be filed in the Office of Agraria in either the city or the district where the land is located (municipal or rural). For *hak guna usaha* (right of exploitation), applications are to be filed in the Office of Agraria at the provincial level.

At the city/district level the following five steps occur in the registration process:

1. The application is filed.

2. The applicant pays the necessary fees for a letter of measurement and the administrative costs for checking and processing the application.

3. The application is referred to a committee called Committee A (Panitia A) for in-the-field checking, evaluation of the application, and preparation of a report on the land use aspects of the application. Committee A is an ad hoc committee established for this purpose, and it is composed of a representative from Agraria, a representative from the village involved, and other individuals from the area who are familiar with the land. The committee also determines if there are any claims of ownership to the land and makes appropriate recommendations on resolution of conflicts. The committee prepares a report of its findings and submits the report to the head of the city or district office of Agraria.

4. Based on Committee A's report, the agrarian office at the city/ district level prepares a letter of recommendation on whether or not the application should be approved.

5. The letter of recommendation is then sent to the provincial office of Agraria for further action.

For registration at the provincial level there are also five steps to be followed:

1. The application is filed.

2. The applicant pays the necessary fees for a letter of measurement and administrative costs for checking and processing the application.

3. The application is referred to Committee B (Panitia B) for in-the-field checking and evaluation of the application. This committee prepares recommendations on the land-use aspects of the application. In addition, information is obtained on the financial capability of the applicant and the viability of the proposal. Recommendations are also obtained from the district head and from the governor of the province.

4. Based on Committee B's report and the various recommendations, the provincial Office of Agraria prepares a letter of recommendation on whether or not the application should be approved, specifying the terms and conditions to be included in the titling.

5. The letter of recommendation is then sent to the governor of the province for a decision. Decisions (i.e., issuance of title) are limited by the authority delegated to the governor under the Minister of Home Affairs, Regulation No. 6, 1972. Under this legislation a governor can make decisions within the following limits:

*Hak milik:* If fewer than 2 hectares for agricultural use or if fewer than 2,000 square meters for housing/building use;

*Hak guna bangunan:* If fewer than 2,000 square meters or if up to a maximum of 20 years;

*Hak pakai:* If fewer than 2,000 square meters or if up to a maximum of 10 years;

*Hak Guna Usaha:* If fewer than 25 hectares;

*Hak Pengelolaan:* No authority is given to issue a letter of decision.

All lands in excess of these limits in area and time limitations cannot be approved by the governor and must go to Jakarta for approval by the minister of home affairs. In practice this authority is delegated to the director general of agrarian affairs.

Based on a letter of decision (either from the director general of agrarian affairs or from the governor), the applicant is informed of the decision together with any terms, conditions, and stipulations that are to be included in the title and is advised to pay the remaining amount of fees. A *sertipikat* (certificate of title) is issued and a copy is provided to the applicant with appropriate information (e.g., number of letter of measurement and land book number) being recorded in the official land records.

This process may take anywhere from six months to two to three years with a number of variables affecting the speed of completion. These include efficient survey completion, the lack of both boundary conflicts and protests from other claimants, the provision of complete application information, and the absence of application backlog in any of the agrarian affairs offices.

*Privately Owned Land.* The procedures for applications for registration and titling lands held under title or under *adat* are slightly different. Applications must be filed at the city-district Office of Agraria, and then the following steps must be taken:

1. The applicant pays the fees for the letter of measurement and administrative costs for checking and processing the application.

2. With the application the applicant must include:

   Information on the chronological/historical status of the land- ownership claim(s). This information must be certified by the village head.

   A rough sketch drawing of the land parcel showing boundaries and size. This is prepared and certified from the records of the village by the village head.

   Information on landownership verified by the village head and the subdistrict head.

   Certification and information from the owner/claimant of evidence of payment of taxes. For this verification is required from the village head and the subdistrict head and is based on a verification of tax payments from the tax records.

3. The information submitted is verified by the Office of Agraria with a field check that determines boundaries and to identify any adverse claims to the land.

4. After checking, the land is officially surveyed and the map of the survey is prepared.

5. On completion of the map a copy of the map and verification of ownership/application information are posted in the office of the village head and in the Office of Agraria. The posting allows the public a 60 day period to protest the application and/or boundary information.

6. If at the end of the 60 day period no protests are filed and the application is in order, the Office of Agraria prepares a letter of recommendation on whether the application should be approved. If protests are filed, the applicant, the village head, and the Office of Agraria try to resolve the conflicts. If the protests are valid, the application is rejected and returned to the applicant. If the protests are not valid, processing of the application continues.

7. The letter of recommendation is then sent to the provincial Office of Agraria for issuance of a letter of decision.

8. The applicant is informed of the decision together with terms and conditions that are to be included in the title, and he or she is advised to pay the remaining fees due.

9. On payment of fees a certificate of title is issued and a copy provided to the applicant. The official land records are appropriately noted.

*Certification of Land.* The evidence of legal ownership, based on title and measurement evidence, is called a certificate (*sertipikat*). The certificate consists of a copy of the land book and a copy of the letter of measurement bound together as one document. In cases where a certificate is necessary but the measurement/map has not been completed, a temporary certificate (*sertipikat sementara*) may be issued. Both types of certificates have full legal sufficiency.

Certificates of title are issued for all types of rights (e.g., *hak milik, hak guna bangunan,* or *hak pakai*) on both private- and state-owned land regardless of the type of right (e.g., ownership or lease). It is also possible to have several certificates issued on the same parcel of land that indicate different title interests. The established records system provides the means both for numerical cross-referencing of all such certificates and for issuing/canceling certificates when parcels of land are divided and/or combined into smaller or larger units.

**Socioeconomic Benefits of Land Registration.** The BAL was aimed at introducing a comprehensive land law as well as rationalizing previous legislation. The reform was clearly needed and it has had major socioeconomic benefits. These benefits have arisen out of the nature of land and of land use in Indonesia where the demand for land has become more intense each year as the population has expanded and the land base has remained unchanged. The ratio of people to land is already extremely high in many areas of Indonesia, with Java being the major example: Its population density is 690 per square kilometer, and approximately 62 percent of Indonesia's population of 160 million resides on only 6.9 percent of the land area. Farms in Indonesia are also very small, with the overall average size, excluding estates, of just under 1 hectare. Java has also seen a tendency toward rapid increases in absentee ownership, most notably by the urban elites, allied with an increasing demand for land. Prime agricultural land is in demand for residences, industrial sites, and infrastructure as the country develops. Thus, a system of land registration such as the one introduced by the BAL clearly had major benefits to the three main groups: the individual registrants, the public and the government, and the government development projects that in the New Order period have played such a prominent role in Indonesian life.

Among the benefits to the individual registrants is security of ownership. A certificate provides the landowner with strong evidence backed by the government that he or she has a certain legal right to the land. It provides the owner protection against challenges to ownership and with the satisfaction of knowing that he or she is free to use, develop, conserve, and manage the land to enjoy the fruits of his or her labor. Unfortunately, owing to the still strong influence of *adat* many landowners still feel secure with the *adat* claim of ownership and do not see the land certificate as being of major importance.

Another benefit is access to credit.[3] Borrowers in the major Indonesian credit program, the Bimbingan Massal (Bimas), are required for larger loans to have a letter from the land office stating that the land certification is in progress. This certificate allows the land to be pledged as collateral. Private lenders in some instances also require certificates.

Land registration facilitates orderly land transfer. The BAL requires that all land transferred be registered. Land registration makes it legally clear what rights are being bought and sold or inherited. Registration also makes public any encumbrances on the land title. There is also some indication that a certificate increases the bargaining power of the seller and the market value of the land. This could be of benefit to the small landowner who is forced to sell his or her land to satisfy a pawn or other indebtedness. At the same time, although there is concern that possession of a certificate might make it easier to transfer land and thus increase the rate at which small landowners are selling to large landowners or speculators, a certificate also provides the basis for compensation by the government for land taken for public purposes.

Land registration can resolve boundary disputes between individuals and between individuals and the state because registration establishes legal boundaries. This is important in all parts of Indonesia but particularly in the areas undergoing rapid development, including urban and transmigration areas.

Registration provides a public record. A complete land registration system would help the orderly transfer of thousands of parcels of land and thus improve the efficiency of economic activities and development. Disputes and litigation concerning land would be greatly reduced, resulting in less work for the courts.

Finally, it assists in mortgage credit to the individual registrant. A complete land registration system would be of great benefit to both the government and the private mortgage busines. This aspect would become even more important as Indonesia develops. Thus, as agriculture develops and becomes more capital intensive, as the value of land increases, and as credit possibilities expand, there will be an increasing need throughout the economy to have legal proof of land ownership.

The benefits of land registration to the public and the government include fuller public control of land. It is recognized in Indonesia that private land ownership must be restricted in some instances to provide for a greater public good, and in this aspect, land registration can help provide the tools to control land use. Agraria regulations require that every grant of right on land (e.g., certificate of ownership, rights of exploitation) or permit to alter the use of land must be accompanied by a land-use recommendation. The recommendation is based on evaluation of the condition of the land use, soil fertility/capability, water supply, possible impact of land use to surrounding areas, master plan and company's ground land, socioeconomic aspects of land cultivation, and principle aspects of land use. Consequently, land registration provides the government with a major tool to encourage well-planned land use.

Land registration provides a land ownership database. A comprehensive and complete land registration system can provide the Government of Indonesia with invaluable information for making land policy decisions. A properly designed database can provide statistics on landownership distribution, trends in parcel size, trends in number of hectares per landowner, rate of land transfer (to and for whom), trends in numbers made landless, trends in land-use conversions, and trends in land market value. A land register can be automated and combined with other information such as land use, population, and agricultural census data to provide a complete database for development planning. Once the information is provided and processed, statistical summaries can be generated quickly by various administrative levels such as the village, district, and province.

Another benefit to the public and the government is that the location and hectarage of estate, village, and other public lands are legally established. As the boundaries of private land are determined and ownership is registered, there is residual land that no private individual claims. These areas may include riverbeds and -banks, islands, swamps, or steep rock hillsides. It is essential that the government know the locations and extent of these areas to provide for their management and disposition. This includes issuance of rights of way, easements, and concessions to private individuals and companies.

Land registration assists the government in enforcing land reform. Here, an effective registration system can help enforce the limit on size of ownership and of absentee ownership. In the case of ownership size, the number of hectares a household can control through ownership, land pledge (pawn), or lease is controlled by the land reform regulation under the BAL. The limitation imposed on the maximum size of landholdings has the effect of helping to equalize access to land with the government's compensating the landowner for excess holdings and reselling the land to the smaller landowner on installment payments.

Assistance in improving land tax administration is the final benefit to the public and the government. The size of a parcel is estimated in many cases in a very crude fashion by the land tax (Iuran Pembangunan Daerah, IPEDA) system and is best termed a *tax cadastre*. The legal cadastre established by Agraria provides a more precise measurement of the parcel. When the system is finally fully implemented, an individual's taxes could change with more precise measurement of size using the legal cadastre. At the same time, the eventual replacement of the tax cadastre could reduce the high administrative costs of operating the present dual cadastre system and thus improve IPEDA tax revenues.

The benefits of an adequate land registration system to government development projects include support of transmigration projects. Land registration supports the large government transmigration program by early investigation of land rights, surveys and planning of parcels, and eventual registration of a restricted title in the outer islands areas that in the 1980s were seeing an inflow of up to 100,000 or more transmigrants a year.

Support for special irrigation projects is the second benefit to government development projects. Land registration assists in the development of the many government-funded irrigation projects throughout the country by identifying land rights and surveying ownerships.

Land registration also provides support for other public works projects and planning. Land registration provides special land rights investigations, surveys, and titling for sites and rights of way needed for public purposes. It also provides aerial photographs, ground surveys, and maps generated by land registration for local and regional planning.

Support for the resolution of special problems is the final benefit to government development projects. Out of the mainstream of general land registration, land rights investigations, surveys, and titling are provided in special problem areas. These can include areas where unauthorized occupancy has occurred, particularly on the borders with other countries or where the growing phenomenon of spontaneous transmigration is occurring.

*Implementation of the BAL*

Although the BAL was introduced in 1950, little action was taken in the next few years for a number of reasons. One reason was simply the lack of up-to-date cadastral registration data on the number of minimum and maximum landholdings and on the number of landless farmers and laborers. It was not until 1961, with the results coming out in late 1962, that the first fully comprehensive population census in Indonesia's history, utilizing a 1 percent sample was carried out.[4] In addition, an agricultural census was carried out in 1963, and the results came out in 1964 and 1965.

Both these censuses provided some but not all of the necessary database that would be required to implement the BAL fully. However, the agricultural census unfortunately did not deal directly with land ownership but only with the number of farmers. The data from this census probably also suffered from two other weaknesses. One was the unwillingness of many owners to report their full landholdings because of the new land reform legislation. A second was that the rich farmer who usually owned the best lands, being descendants of the founders of the village, had begun again in light of the land reform to divide their large plots of land among close relatives.

The 1963 population census was unfortunately incomplete because it did not count house compounds and gardens of less than 0.1 hectare, which totaled about 10 percent of farmland in Java (Montgomery 1975, p. 39). A second factor was the lack of macropolicy backing for land reform. An Economic Development Plan (1956–1960) that was just coming to an end when the BAL was introduced in 1960 had had very little to say about agrarian reform. Its successor, the new Eight-Year Development Plan (1961–1968), did refer to agrarian reform and provided some general guidelines for agricultural development but suffered from being a far too general document that had little practical impact in terms of providing clear guidelines for enforcing new policy directions such as those involved in the BAL.

Just as important were other events in these years that moved attention away from agrarian reform. One was Indonesia's political and military moves to gain control of the large area of West Irian from the Dutch government as well as the country's confrontation with Malaysia. Both events disrupted the normal domestic activities at this time. Unfortunately for the implementation of the BAL, once the West Irian dispute was virtually settled, toward the end of 1962, the Malaysian confrontation had become a major issue that was diverting attention from internal policies. In fact, the only factor that helped to keep the whole matter of agrarian reform alive at this time was the intense interest of the active Indonesian Communist party in these years in ensuring its implementation specifically in terms of land redistribution. By far the most influential political party in terms of grass-roots activities, the Indonesian Communist party was to keep land reform and its implementation moving until the party was eliminated wholesale after the 1965 abortive coup that marked the start of the New Order period.[5]

The bureaucratic machinery that existed at that time was typically slow even if it was functioning properly. The Department of Agrarian

Affairs, which was responsible for the implementation of land reform, was weak. Coordination among the various departments involved in land reform—such as those of public works and power, cooperatives and transmigration, agriculture, and home affairs—was inadequate. Finally, the already existing strong position of the leadership in village bureaucracies was not changed by the land reform legislation, and not surprisingly, the vested interests of the village leaders, including their ownership of the better parts of land in their village areas, led to their lack of compliance in most cases with the new land reform legislation.

Given this background three main activities can be discerned in the execution of the land reform regulations from the beginning of 1961 to the end of 1965: the registration of the land, the determination of the existing surplus and its distribution to as many landowners as possible, and the implementation of the 1960 law (Law No. 2 of 1960) on sharecropping agreements. Initially, however, the administrative structure for land reform had to be set up. This was done through the setting up of the land reform committees formed under Presidential Decree No. 131 of 1961 to assess and distribute surplus land. These committees were arranged in hierarchical order, a central committee under the guidance of the president, the provincial committees under the chair of the governors, the district committees under the respective district heads, the subdistrict under the subdistrict heads, and the village committees under the village administration. The district committees were the most important committees since they had to do the actual work such as surveying and measuring the land, assessing land surplus, determining compensation to be paid to the landowners, composing lists of persons eligible for allotments, and settling disputes.

The procedures to be followed in redistributing the land and in assessing and paying the indemnifications were laid down in a government regulation (No. 224 of 1961), and the land reform committees started their work on September 1, 1961. It took, however, a year of preparatory activities before the activities of reform could be started on September 24, 1962. Thus, it was not until 1963 that the first lists of land areas available for redistribution, totaling 337,000 hectares of excess land, were submitted to the government by the district committees in Java, Madura, Bali, and Lombok. This figure was much lower than the 966,150 hectares initially estimated in 1961 (Indonesia, Minister of Agrarian Affairs, 1965, p. 7) for the first stage of implementation in Java, Madura, Bali, and NTB (Nusa Tenggora Barat or West Nusa Tenggora) but did represent a more realistic figure based on the work of the district committee.

Overall redistribution of land was to be carried out in two stages, first in Java, Madura, Bali, and NTB, where the distribution of land surplus together with the distribution of land of former native kingdoms (*tanah swapraja*) was to be finished by the end of 1963 or early in 1964. This was to be followed by stage two, covering Sumatra, Kalimantan, Sulawesi, and the rest of the country. According to the Eight-Year Development Plan (1961–1968) approved by the National Assembly in December 1960, the whole process of redistribution was to be finished within 3 to 5 years. This was not to take place, however, for the reasons already given and also because of the compromise nature of the BAL. One of the major weaknesses of the final BAL was the levels of maximum and minimum ownership. these limits had been reached by taking into account the representations of the peasants and laborers who wanted a system of allowing land only to those who actually worked it (*sistim paragrap*) and those who had traditional property rights in land (*milik atas tanah*). This latter group were mostly representatives of religious organizations who argued that according to Indonesian traditional law the land was inalienable (Utrecht 1969, pp. 72–73).

As a result, the interests of the landowner were given considerable weight, and the maximum holdings were relatively high. As the World Bank noted, "under Javanese conditions fixing the ceiling at 5 ha for Java was flying in the face of reality" (World Bank 1974, p. 37). There were also many loopholes for eluding the prohibitions on absenteeism and for keeping lands outside the range of the land reform. If in fact the landholding size had been lowered and there had been harsher treatment for the recorded total of 60,000 absentee landowners, even on Java, Madura, and Bali where the landholdings were fewer in number in terms of size, it has been estimated that it would have been possible to create a land surplus double this size. This certainly would have provided more land for distribution to the estimated 3 million landless in 1960 (Utrecht 1976, p. 78). Other weaknesses in the BAL that hampered its implementation were well summarized in a report by the Minister of Agrarian Affairs in January 1964. The report included the following points:

Deficiencies in the registration of land hampered investigations of the land surplus and opened the way to abuses.

The lack of understanding of the necessity and significance of land reform as an instrument of social change among wide sections of the people made it easier for landlords to obstruct the reforms.

There was insufficient cooperation among the members of the committees, partly because other duties kept some of them from devoting their full attention to the tasks of the committees and partly because many of the committee members were interested in the failure of land reform. The peasants' organizations, which should have lent the strongest support to reform, were prevented from playing a significant part on the committees.

The peasants were still subject to strong psychological and economic pressure from the landowners that kept them from pushing for an efficient execution of land reform.

It proved difficult to establish an order of priority in redistributing land either because many fields had no regular laborers or because, through changes in registration, the workers concerned had been listed as absentees. Such cases resulted in severe disputes between landowners and laborers or among the laborers that, in turn, often gave rise to quarrels among various political organizations. (Indonesia, Minister of Agrarian Affairs 1964, pp. 11–12)

To this list must be added the fact that the government aroused the suspicion among the landowners that they would not be adequately compensated for the land taken for land redistribution. The government had promised from the beginning that it would buy surplus land at a fair price and resell it at the same price with the provision of credit to new owners, but it soon became clear in the early years that this promise was not being kept. Consequently, the suspicion of the landowners, fanned by interested political organizations, led to considerable resistance to the new legislation. To some extent this resistance was allayed by the proclamation of the Emergency Law No. 3 of 1963 updating the 1961 legislation (Regulation No. 224 of 1961) which laid down clearly the compensation to be paid to landowners. But by February 1968, the record showed that no compensation had been received by any of the former landowners with the exception of a small payment made in the regency of Bandung and Bali (Utrecht 1976, p. 279).

Finally, an additional problem in introducing land reform in Indonesia was the rather complicated legislation. This became fully articulated by a considerable number of laws, decrees, and regulations, all promulgated between 1960 and 1964 and each dealing with specific issues. Thus, the initial Law No. 2 of 1960 dealt only with the sharecropping problem. During 1960 laws implementing the basic BAL principles and also the limits on the maximum holdings of agricultural land were issued. These were followed by Law No. 1 of 1961 that addressed the serious problem of land owned by very small landholders but controlled through indebtedness by moneylenders or wealthy farmers. This law stipulated that after paying interest for 7 years the official owner of land could get back his or her land. Then there were regulations about the implementation of the reform program that started to come out in 1961. These regulations covered the setting up of land reform committees under Presidential Decree No. 131 of 1961 and were followed by the regulations covering various aspects of implementation. These included Regulation No. 224 of September 1961, which covered redistribution of land in excess of the minimum limit, of the land of absentee owners, and of the land of principalities and absent principalities. At the same time there were a number of problems with the legislation, particularly in relation to absentee landholders and shareholdings.

Absentee landholders were defined as owners who reside outside the subdistrict in which their lands are located. They had to transfer their land to inhabitants of that subdistrict, or it would be taken over by the government under Regulation No. 224 of 1961. The number of absentee landholders was not large, totaling only 60,000 in the area of Java, Madura, and Bali covered by stage one (Indonesia, Minister of Agrarian Affairs 1965). In practice, they were treated very leniently, with only 8,600 hectares of a total of 22,000 hectares belonging to 18,000 absentee landowners finally distributed in the first phase (Huizer 1974, p. 84). This lenience may well have been due to the lack of clarity in the legislation; namely, the definition of absenteeism was open to interpretation.

Shareholding raised two problems in the implementation of the BAL. One problem was the Gadai system in which small landowners placed their land at the disposition of the creditors in exchange for loans and the creditors were able to use the land until the debt had been repaid. Many large farm units were composed of plots controlled under this system, and it was unclear who exactly owned what. A second problem arose when the land of an owner of a number of plots was being worked by sharecroppers and thus did not figure as one farmholding in the statistics except where the owner worked the plot directly him- or herself or with farmhands. Law No. 2 of 1960 attempted to deal directly with this ownership problem by limiting sharecropping. In the case of Gadai, Law No. 1 of 1961 stipulated that after getting interest for 7 years the official owner of the land could automatically get back the land in the hope that this would deal with this problem. In practice, this solution did not work because the sharecroppers were reluctant to return the land after the old contracts between themselves and the owners had terminated. This happened in 1964/1965 on a large scale and led to Regulation No. 4 of March 1964, which attempted to lay down a fairer basis for sharecropping that, it was argued, until then was too much in the landlord's favor. Thus, with this regulation the division of the harvest would be 60 percent of the harvest for the tiller, 20 percent for the landlord, and 20 percent for the *kecamatan* (subdistrict) land reform committee.

46 · *Land Policy in Modern Indonesia*

**Table 2.1.**
**Land Distribution and Number of Beneficiaries Under**
**Land Reform from 1960–1969**

| Area | Land Distributed (Hectares) | Number of Bene- ficiaries | Average Plot (Hectares) | Land Category (Percentage) |
|---|---|---|---|---|
| Indonesia | 682,000 | 867,000 | 0.8 | 17 percent excess and absentee land |
| | | | | 83 percent ex-state-controlled land including principalities |
| Java | 294,000 | 592,958 | 0.5 | 25 percent excess and absentee land |
| Outer Islands | 388,198 | 274,025 | 1.4 | 11 percent excess and absentee land |
| Total | 1,364,198 | 1,733,983 | | |

*Source:* Tjondronegoro (1972).

Looking at the statistics of land reform in the early years, one see how little was achieved. The land to be redistributed consisted of excess holdings, state-controlled land, and formal principalities. The largest areas of land were state-controlled land consisting of 1.4 million hectares with excess landholdings, according to the 1963 agricultural census (Indonesia, Bureau of Statistics 1963), totaling some 725,000 hectares. This figure is higher than that submitted to the government through the village and district committees due probably to underregistration at the various levels. By 1965 the total of state-controlled land redistributed came to only 454,966 hectares, which was allocated to 568,862 people. The sizable portion of this type of land, consisting of some 165,000 hectares mostly in North Sumatra, remained undistributed (Tjondronegoro 1972, p. 7).

In terms of redistribution of excess lands, only some 55 to 60 percent were distributed up to 1969, and much of the land redistributed in the early years from 1965 through 1969 was to be reclaimed by the landlords in subsequent years. This was particularly noticeable in the post-1965 coup period when the reverse of land distribution occurred: Distribution virtually stopped in 1966 and 1967, and an estimated 150,000 hectares reverted back (Utrecht 1969, p. 81). In 1968 things began to move more smoothly, but a new factor entered into the process when the army began to act as brokers or to demand land for their civil mission (Operasi Karya) activities (Utrecht 1969, p. 87). At the same time the New Order government that came to power in 1965 did not have the political and ideological interests in land reform of the Old Order, which had focused its attention more on economic development. Overall, as Table 2.1 shows, land distributed under land reform up to 1969 totaled some 1.3 million hectares, benefiting approximately 1.7 million farmers.

## Notes

1. A landowner may control any number of parcels in the district if each one is under the 2 hectare limitation, but under no circumstances may he or she control more than five parcels if the parcels are located both in the subdistrict of residence and the adjoining subdistrict.
2. For a detailed description, see Minister of Home Affairs Regulation No. 72 of 1981, outlining the organization of the Department of Home Affairs in Jakarta including the Directorate General of Agrarian Affairs. In the 1960s there was a separate Department for Land Affairs (*Departemen Agraria*) that in the 1970s was moved under the Department of Home Affairs (*Departemen Dalam Negeri*).
3. See Appendix B for details of existing credit systems, their requirements, and how these might be closely linked to land certification in the future.
4. The first population census, which was very incomplete, had been carried out in 1931. There is a lack of reliable data even for the 1960s with sometimes conflicting sets of figures.
5. For detailed discussion of this period, the role of the Communist party and its collapse as a political force in Indonesian life, see Rex Mortimer (Ed.): Indonesia, *Showcase State*, Angus & Robertson Sydney 1973 and Rex Mortimer 'The Place of Communism' in E. McVay (Ed.) *Studies in Indonesia History*, Pitmans Victoria 1976.

# 3

---

# Land Policy in the
# New Order Period

## National Plans and Programs

With the coming to power of the New Order government in 1965/1966, Indonesian politics and national policies were both to undergo radical shifts. It took the New Order government some time to establish its authority initially in the chaotic conditions that it faced in the first few years of its rule, but once it did it devoted its energies to the economic development of the country. This involved the immediate need to bring law and order to the country, to rebuild the infrastructure and the economy that by 1966 were both badly in need of repair, and to develop and sustain a series of consistent development policies. Thus, the priorities were to stabilize the economy, to build up the industrial base, to create employment, and above all, to become self-sustaining in the agricultural field. The last aim led to the introduction of a number of major government programs to support the agriculture sector, including the now famous Bimas and Inmas programs for the intensification of crops, particularly that of rice;[1] a series of rural works programs; and the transmigration program that attempted to deal with the overpopulation problem on Java by moving people from Java to the outer islands as well as to assist in the general development of the outer islands.

The major guidelines for government policy during the New Order period were set out in the Guidelines for National Policy (GBHN) announced before each five-year national development plan and then incorporated into the five-year development plans. Each plan, starting with the First Five-Year Development Plan (1969/1970–1973/1974) to the most recent Fourth Five-Year Development Plan (1984/1985–1988/ 1989), laid down a series of priorities that changed as matters improved in the country over the years but all have related to the underlying priority of building and sustaining a sound economy and developing self-sufficiency in agriculture.

In the First Five-Year Development Plan, the emphasis was on infrastructure rehabilitation; on agriculture extension including the extensive distribution of fertilizers, seed, and pesticides; and on installing adequate monetary controls in the country to bring down the very high inflation rate. Infrastructure in particular was badly in need of rehabilitation. Little had been done since independence because of the changing conditions and pressures within the country, and it was of immediate importance that the existing infrastructure be repaired and a new infrastructure provided as a basis for rebuilding the country. The agriculture sector was seen quite rightly as the primary government investment priority in this First Five-Year Plan. The main aim was that of achieving self-sufficiency in rice production, an effort that was seen as entailing an increase of approximately 50 percent in domestic output. This was to be done by using a new high-yielding rice that was developed through a different mix of seeds from the Green Revolution, which swept Asia in the late 1960s and introduced new varieties of seeds. The increase in rice production was helped also by providing central production inputs, particularly those of fertilizers and credit, which had been lacking for years. Many of these activities were incorporated into the Bimas campaign, a national agricultural intensification program involving the fusion of inputs (credit, seed, and fertilizers) needed for the successful cultivation of the new high-yielding varieties.

Most Bimas activities were centered on Java, and at its highest point in 1974–1975, this program covered a large proportion of the island's lowland rice-growing areas. By the end of the First Five-Year Development Plan, the Bimas program had been markedly successful, and although it was to slow down later, it showed that the goal of rice self-sufficiency was feasible (Hansen 1981, p. 10). With the Second Five-Year Development Plan (1974/1975–1978/1979) the focus moved to that of employment generation for small farmers, landless laborers, and small-scale labor involved in the public works programs. In seeking to stimulate employment opportunities in the rural sector during this five-year period, three programs emerged that were to become a major feature of Indonesia's development policies in the 1970s. These were the Kabupaten Program, the Padat Karya Program, and the Subsidy Desa Program.

The Kabupaten (district) Program, started in 1970, sought to foster greater local government initiative at the district level in the financing of public works projects. The aim was to provide labor-intensive construction projects administered by individual district governments with additional central government funds being provided as an incentive for those districts that performed well in the collection of local taxes, a strategy that greatly improved district-level performance in meeting their tax collection targets.

The Padat Karya (rural works) Program was aimed at improving rural infrastructure and generating more employment opportunities in the rural sector. It was administered by the subdistrict level of government that stands between the district and the village. It brought local development activity into the closest proximity with the villagers, creating short-term employment for the rural poor during the slack agriculture season and involving laborers in the construction of small-scale infrastructure projects that would generate long-term gains. Starting on a small scale in 1969, it had become by the mid-1970s a countrywide program that was achieving significant results.

The third program associated with the government's attempt to improve welfare levels within the rural sector was the Subsidy Desa (village subsidy) Program. This consisted of an annual grant from the central government to each village in Indonesia for village-level infrastructure projects. Initiated in 1969, the amount has been increased every year and by 1985/1986 totaled $1,200 per village (*Kompas*, February 2, 1986, p. 3). The intent of these allocations was to mobilize greater local participation in the development process, and thus, the funding was limited to the purchase of construction materials not available in the local village and the labor was donated by the village.

These programs underline the importance placed in the 1970s on intensive employment-generating projects in the public works sector. A fourth, more agriculturally focused, program, the Penghijauan and Reboisasi (regreening and rehabilitation) Program, was aimed at increasing incomes and employment for low-income rural groups by helping the rehabilitation of areas suffering from severe soil erosion. In upland Java, for instance, erosion was such a serious problem that nearly 80 percent of all *kabupatens* in the upland areas had erosion problems (Hansen 1981, p. 17). This program, launched in 1975, helped combat this problem while also utilizing sizable labor inputs and creating additional employment opportunities.

While most of these programs focused on the densely populated areas of Java, the outer islands areas benefited from the government's policies of encouraging agricultural diversification, rural industry, and transmigration to the outer islands. The focus of policy in the outer islands areas usually was on the opening up of new areas for development and cropping aimed at bringing these historically neglected and isolated areas into the mainstream of Indonesia's development. The Indonesian trans-migration program that by the early 1980s had moved between 3 million and 4 million people, both under the government-sponsored program and through spontaneous movement, became a major force in developing new areas in the outer islands such as Sumatra, Sulawesi, Kalimantan, and Irian Jaya (MacAndrews 1978). Although the initial aim of the program was to relieve population pressure in Java, it became more and more focused in the 1970s on stimulating greater agriculture productivity in the outer islands areas and thus contributing to the resources of the country both internally and in terms of exports.

## Land Policy

Throughout the New Order period, priority, as we have seen, was given to the overall economic development of the country and, in particular, to the development of the agriculture sector. Consequently, land reform and redistribution that had been so important a part of government policy in the 1960s was relegated to the background. Practically all government efforts in the agriculture sector were now going into for-mulating appropriate pricing policies for inputs and outputs and to rehabilitating and extending rural infrastructure. The official govern-ment attitude to land reform under the New Order was that in Java and Bali holdings were already too small and fragmented for land reform to be of any relevance as a rural development strategy. In this regard the policymakers were correct. Indonesia and Java in particular certainly did not fall into any of the categories that usually indicate urgent need for land reform. It did not, for instance, suffer from the usual feudal Asian type of landownership and land use characterized by a high prop-erty concentration, great social and economic inequality, and operation mainly by sharecroppers (World Bank 1975). In fact, the opposite was true in many of Indonesia's large outer islands areas, with their wide-spread traditional communal type of land tenure involving low property concentration and with sovereign rights being vested in the community.

The growing awareness of the problem of providing productive work for the rural landless in Java resulted in some continuing interest in the question of agrarian reform. One of the most interesting proposals that was put forward in this period was one by the noted Indonesian scholar, Sajogyo (1977). He suggested that the help the government gave to farmers through the Bimas and BUUD (Badan Usaha Unit Desa) prog-rams could be extended to cooperatives for the near-landless and agricul-tural laborers. Farmers owning less than 0.2 hectare and all landless households in rural Java and elsewhere in Indonesia would be encouraged to join the cooperatives, and the government would compensate those farmers who contributed their land to communal use. Sajogyo also suggested that more realistic land ceilings be applied than those provided under the 1960 BAL and that those farmers owning more than the maximum, including the *bengkok* landholding of village officials,[2] would have to surrender their excess land. Although this scheme was attractive, there were obvious difficulties in implementing it. Rough calculations based on the 1973 Agricultural Census (Indonesia, Bureau of Statistics 1973) suggest that if all the holdings below 0.2 hectare in Java were added to all landholdings in excess of 2 hectares, there would be only about 900,000 hectares of land to redistribute. This clearly is too little land to support even the 1.8 million smallholders operating in the 1970s with less than 0.2 hectare, let alone those who were landless.

Unfortunately, if there was a concern to provide work for the rural landless, there did not appear to be in the 1970s any sharp downturn in income that would have helped bring about greater pressure for agrarian reform. There was admittedly in this period clearly an increase in expenditure disparities between the urban and the rural areas of Java allied with substantial landlessness in the rural areas (White 1978). The number of people dependent on the agriculture sector also declined in the 1970s and early 1980s, a decline that was allied with a substantial technological labor displacement (World Bank 1985, p. 106). But in spite of these changes, real expenditure in both the urban and the rural areas of Java increased between 1970 and 1984 for all deciles of the population. In the agriculture sector this was due to a great extent to the favorable prices for farmers, significant productivity increases, and the greater proportion of nonagriculture incomes.

It is clear that the development strategy pursued by the New Order government in the 1970s did not lead to any rapid increase in income disparities or in the number of people in absolute poverty anywhere in the country. If there was some evidence of increasing urban disparities in Java, there was little evidence of growing disparities in other areas of the country, particularly in the rural areas. As Table 3.1 illustrates for a sample of villages in West Java, the real household income and therefore purchasing power increased for all classes of farmers. There was also a marked increase in incomes from nonagricultural sources for the landless, who constitute a large portion of the total population in rural Java. This allowed them to increase their real expenditure at the same pace as other groups in rural society.

The diversification into nonagricultural activities was also evident among both medium and large farmers. While they did not diversify as

**Table 3.1.**
**Household Income by Economic Class, West Java Villages,
1976 and 1983**

| Group | Share of Households in Survey (%) | Average Household Income[a] (Thousands of Rupiahs) | | Average Growth 1976–1983 (% Per Annum) |
|---|---|---|---|---|
| | | 1976 | 1983 | |
| Landless[b] | | | | |
| Farm laborers | 10 | 224 | 310 | 4.7 |
| Nonagricultural | 5 | 461 | 642 | 4.8 |
| Farmers | | | | |
| Small (less than 0.25 ha) | 40 | 402 | 498 | 3.1 |
| Medium (0.25–0.5 ha) | 23 | 421 | 610 | 5.5 |
| Large (greater than 0.5 ha) | 23 | 710 | 884 | 3.1 |
| All households | 100 | 464 | 602 | 3.8 |

*Source:* Agro-Economic Survey, Rural Labor Market Surveys, West Java, 1977 and 1984.
[a] All 1976 data is in 1983 prices.
[b] Classified by major source of household income.

much into nonfarm activities, small farmers increased their incomes in this period. Thus, small and what are often perceived as inadequate landholdings were clearly not a constraint on agricultural growth (World Bank 1985, p. 13). Viewed against this background, the need for land distribution as a means of directly aiding the rural poor lost much of its urgency.

## Land Use

### Rural Land Use

It is interesting to see the kind of changes that occurred in rural land use between 1963 and 1973, a period for which Indonesia has two major agricultural censuses that have been fully analyzed and published. Given the changes in the country during this decade, one would expect, with the very small farm size (particularly on Java) and the rapid population increase, that small-to-medium size farms would become increasingly smaller through inheritance and land transfer related to indebtedness and that all arable land would, particularly on Java, be agriculturally exploited. One would also expect that dry agricultural land would have been widely converted to *sawah* and that there would be evidence of greater inequality in landholdings.[4]

Comparison of these two censuses shows some interesting results (Indonesia, Bureau of Statistics 1963, 1973). One is that total land use did not increase as expected in Java and Bali, that there was an increase in small farm holdings, that the expected decrease in size of the small and medium farms did not occur, and that where there was a considerable change in land use, it occurred outside Java, particularly in Sumatra with the conversion of dry land to *sawah*.

In Java and Bali, the lack of a marked increase in land use was due to the very limited land available for cultivation. There was, however, a marked increase in small farm holdings, particularly those operating *sawah*. This reflected the increase in overall land use: Agricultural land use throughout Indonesia was growing at an annual rate of 0.74 percent a year as opposed to a growth rate of 1.72 percent a year for *sawah*. While the growth of *sawah* was at the expense of dry land, it is interesting to note that the conversion was far greater, both in terms of size and of the annual rate of conversion, in the outer islands—in particular, on Sumatra more than on Java and Bali. The increase in *sawah* in these traditionally swidden agricultural areas was probably due to the national transmigration program's role in developing agriculturally the outer islands. There was no evidence in the censuses of any decrease of small farms or of the small farmer being squeezed out by agricultural circumstances (Montgomery 1975, p. 14). Larger farms (more than 5 hectares) in fact decreased in number both for dry land and *sawah* Finally, there was no evidence of extensive renting out; the 1973 agricultural census (Bureau of Statistics 1973) showed that the majority of farms was completely owned by the operator.

This period also saw little change in the pattern of landlessness. Indonesia ranks near the bottom in terms of the number of farms being operated by persons who own no part of the land they operate (3.2 percent) in contrast to roughly compatible countries such as Thailand (4.1 percent) and South Korea (6.7 percent) and to the very high rates found in India (16.9 percent), Ceylon (32.6 percent), and the Philippines (39.9 percent). In no major agricultural island of Indonesia was the percentage of farms that were not completely owned by the operator in this period below 69 percent (Montgomery 1975, p. 21), and in Indonesia's rural areas inequality of either landholdings or incomes is not the serious problem that it is in other Asian countries.

If the comparison of the censuses shows these kinds of structural changes in land use and ownership in this period, they are due in part to one major government program, the Indonesian transmigration program, that has played and will continue to play an important role in developing and changing the agriculture patterns in the outer islands.

Moving some 3 million to 4 million people either directly or spontaneously from Java to the outer islands, the transmigration program has led to an increase in intensified cultivation in many of the outer islands areas. This is particularly notable in the two major outer islands areas of Sumatra and of South Sulawesi where a significant move from dry land farming to *sawah* was allied with double cropping and intensification. Given the large number of farmers moved under the transmigration program, with even larger numbers projected to be moved in the Fourth Five-Year Plan period (1984/1985–1988/1989), the program has had considerable impact on the outer islands areas, particularly in the transfer of Javanese agricultural practices. Whether these practices are particularly appropriate to the outer islands is a matter of debate (Dove 1986), but their impact cannot be ignored.

Under the transmigration program land is prepared in the outer islands areas for residential and agricultural purposes through the clearing of forest or the reclaiming of swamp land. Initially, land surveys are carried out, project boundaries are measured, the surveying is done, and the individual settled plots of land are provided with titles. Although the aims of the transmigration program are officially stated as helping to relieve the population pressure on Java and the development of the outer islands areas, its role of raising national agricultural productivity has also become a major goal of the program in recent years, reflecting the realization of the significant contribution that the program can make in this area (MacAndrews 1978). The effectiveness of the program in the various areas and its impact on population redistribution have been analyzed elsewhere (World Bank 1985; Babcock 1986). What is of particular interest in terms of land policy is this program's impact on land use and agricultural practices in the newly opened areas.

In looking at the impact of transmigration settlement on the outer islands areas, one can see that by 1983 some 60,000 square kilometers of forest swampland and grassland had been cleared and put under cultivation by the settlers (Babcock 1986, p. 9). Considerably more of this total had been distributed to the settlers in the form of uncleared land to be developed by the settlers, although this land has always been much slower in coming into production. The influence of the transmigration program on land use is well demonstrated if one compares the amount of transmigrant land cultivated with the total amount of land under cultivation in the individual provinces. This kind of comparison shows that almost 26 percent of the land in East Kalimantan, 23 percent in Southeast Sulawesi, 21 percent in South Sumatra, 18 percent in Jambi, and 16 percent in Bengkulu of the total land under cultivation in 1973 was being worked by transmigrants, reflecting clearly the impact of this particular program on agricultural development and land-use patterns in the outer islands provinces (Babcock 1986, p. 14). In addition, much of this settlement has taken place on land that was agronomically, ecologically, or economically unsuited to usual foodcrop agriculture, and the program has clearly played an important role in opening up new areas for development that would not have been opened under other circumstances. Overall three-quarters of the settlements today throughout Indonesia are located on dry land or upland areas, mostly without irrigation, with soils that are low in nutrients and often acidic.

The effect of this program and the agricultural practices attached to it, originating both from central government policy and from the experience of the predominantly Javanese transmigrants, has been of considerable importance. In these outer islands areas the main type of cultivation historically has been the extensive shifting type, sometimes with a tree crop component, that has been practiced for centuries. This practice is ecologically sound in areas of low population density that exist in the outer islands. The influxes of transmigrants have brought more sedentary forms of agriculture, with fixed plots, leading to a considerable change in agricultural practices with greater emphasis on wet rice *sawah* production in some of the outer islands—notably, Sumatra (Dove 1982; Babcock 1986). Although the benefits of this change in agricultural practices has been questioned, the transmigration program has succeeded in increasing food production to a significant extent in some areas and has started to make a small but valuable contribution to the country's overall agricultural production.

The program, however, has had two negative effects in terms of land-use and land matters. The first is the ecological impact of the settlement programs on the outer islands areas. Many of the ecosystems in Indonesia are notoriously fragile, and the influx of a large number of transmigrant settlers has threatened the stability of those systems. Because erosion control and soil conservation methods were not built into the program, the transmigration has destroyed the natural habitat of many forest creatures and has broken up the traditional local shifting cultivation systems. It has also led to the destruction of vast areas of tropical rain forest, replacing these areas with unsuitable and unstable farming systems. The attention being paid to the ecological effects of the program in the late 1970s by the Indonesian government and international donor agencies involved in supporting the transmigration program is evidence of growing concern. The Minister of Population and the Environment, for instance, began paying special attention in the late 1970s to the ecological aspects of transmigration settlements;

the Department of Agriculture began promoting soil conservation in transmigration areas; and the World Bank, by far the largest international donor supporting the program, started to provide technical assistance to the government to try to identify solutions to these problems.

The second effect of the transmigration program has been the clashes that have resulted from its activities between modern Indonesian law and existing traditional law. Although the BAL of 1960 had clarified the legal relationship of *adat* with modern legal practice in terms of land distribution and land rights, the BAL was still not fully applied throughout the country by the 1980s. Consequently, the existing systems of traditional law in many of the outer islands areas often made the whole process of land development under the transmigration program very difficult (Ross 1984, p. 225). The impact on the local areas of the large number of transmigrant settlers has been considerable and has led to inevitable clashes between the existing traditional rights in the local areas and the rights given to the settler by the government of the land appropriated for transmigration settlement. Thus, in many of the transmigration areas the transmigrants, after the first 1 or 2 difficult years of establishing themselves, find that the local inhabitants come back to claim the land the new inhabitants have cultivated. This situation has applied particularly to land turned into *sawah* and that consequently has provided an attractive area to be reclaimed by the local inhabitants under *adat*. Because *adat* is unwritten and entails no evidence of ownership, these conflicts are difficult to resolve.

*Urban Land Use*

Turning to the urban dimension of land problems, Indonesia in the 1970s was undergoing rapid urban growth at a rate estimated at a minimum of 4 percent a year and expected to continue at this rate in the future (World Bank 1985, pp. iii–v). The urban population between 1970 and 1980 increased from 15 percent to 22 percent of the total population. This increase resulted in new pressure on urban land and growing absentee landlordism in the rural areas, particularly on Java. In addition, the rapid growth of urban areas led to a lack of adequate land in the major cities for housing and government improvement programs. The demand for limited urban land led in turn to higher urban land prices, which affected both individuals and government programs—in particular, public housing schemes. At the same time the lengthy procedures involved in obtaining title to land became one of the main barriers to the ability of both the private and the public sector to meet housing demands. The result is that Indonesia has a particularly low expenditure of only some 3 percent of its GNP on housing in comparison to the more usual level of 5 percent (World Bank 1984, p. XIV).

In 1984 a report in one of the major Indonesian-language papers that had commissioned a survey of urban land problems (*Kompas*, September 12, 1984 p. XII) noted that there were pressing land shortages in most of the country's large cities, particularly those in Java. City development programs, where they did exist, were being outrun by the rapid growth of their populations, particularly in the large cities of Bandung, Surabaya, Bogor, and Semarang on Java. The survey reported that Bandung could accommodate an absolute maximum of 1.72 million people and was already reaching this limit in 1984 with the growing influxes of people every year. A similar situation could be found in Surabaya, the second largest city in the country with a population of 2.5 million people, in which the report noted was that "if anybody needs land the city has hardly any more land to offer" (ibid.). In Jakarta it was reported that all the land in the total Jakarta area would be utilized inside the next 20 years. With a population of 7 million that increases by 4 percent a year, the city alone needed 70,000 new houses a year. Its land pressure was reflected in the enormous increase in land prices from some Rp50,000 ($50) per square meter in 1981 to Rp200,000 ($200) per square meter in 1984 in the same areas. Yet the pressure for land and investment in land seems to continue, in part due to the fact that owning land was seen as a good investment as well as a status symbol (ibid.).

## Land-use Problems

It is not surprising that land problems in both urban and rural areas, reflecting the changes in the country including rapid urbanization, led to constant low-key protests throughout the 1970s and early 1980s by small landholders who had lost their land or had been deprived of ownership in the development of both urban and rural areas.

A survey of Jakarta newspapers in 1985 highlighted a number of problems, some related directly with land reform, others with the issue of land certificates, urban land, and land ownership occurring in transmigration projects.[5] These problems indicate some advancement in applying a system of land certification and in trying to get the land policy as outlined in the BAL implemented, but they also illustrate the generally confused state in a rapidly developing country over the status of land. We discuss some particularly prominent problems in the following subsections.

**Land Certificates.** The delays in issuing land certificates were often commented on. It was estimated that getting a certificate usually takes more than 1 year. Those applying put down the delays to an inefficient bureaucracy and the need to make a number of illegal payments to the offices at various levels involved in the issuance of a certificate. The government stated officially (*Jakarta Post*, September 1, 1984) that it takes only 3 to 6 months to get a certificate but that many of the applications are not fully documented. However, it was acknowledged that there is a lack of adequate personnel to service the certification process in the Agraria offices throughout the country and that many of those already employed are not fully qualified.

Other complaints included the high cost of obtaining land certificates from the Directorate General of Agrarian Affairs, quoted at around Rp100,000 ($100) for each certificate. Without "grease," one report ran (*Jakarta Post*, May 4, 1984), obtaining land certificates was either delayed or did not happen. "The practice," the article noted, "was to pay first with service later." Additional legal fees were charged at each stage, including US$5 to get a number to use in making a registration, another US$10 to get approval of the application, US$25 for the district office, and US$25 for the specific section of the Department of Land Affairs (Agraria) that issues the permit for the use of the land. Then there are extra levies to be paid at the subdistrict office and for typing the certificate.

Despite all these problems, the newspaper reports made clear that certificates were in growing demand. One newspaper (*Jakarta Post*, February 18, 1984) reported that under the PRONA the target of issuing 12,000 certificates for Jakarta had been exceeded: About 24,000 people had applied. A number of reports also indicate that there was a large market in bogus land certificates. One report (*Indonesian Times*, July 15, 1984, p. 3) noted that 180 bogus land certificates had been confiscated by the Jakarta Agrarian Office "because of the doubtful nature of the official signature." This particular phenomenon seems more common in urban areas with the tremendous pressure on land in the large cities of Jakarta, Surabaya, and Bandung than in the rural areas in Indonesia.

Another report (*Jakarta Post*, February 18, 1984) reported that 8,000 of the 15,000 land certificates issued by Jakarta under the PRONA in 1983 had been declared invalid because they had not been processed through government channels, which even a Jakarta Agraria Office spokesman was quoted as saying were "notoriously time consuming." (Ibid., February 8, 1984.) Thus, it would seem that although certificates were not always necessary in land purchases, they were expected by most buyers of land. This, however, did not seem to apply to government land where there was the additional problem of confusion about whether the central or the local government owned the land. As a result of this problem, many of the government buildings in Jakarta did not have land certificates (*Jakarta Post*, July 12, 1984).

**Urban Land Acquisition.** The pressure on land in Indonesia's main cities inevitably created by the late 1970s a whole range of problems. In Jakarta, for instance, constant conflicts were reported between the Jakarta administrators and homeowners whose houses were being taken over for government development. In most of these cases the government argued that the area was illegally occupied and that they had every right to demolish the houses for development. One particularly interesting case that underlines the seriousness of this kind of problem was a lawsuit brought to a North Jakarta court in mid-1984. In this case fifty-three families were represented who were trying to save their houses that were going to be demolished so the area could be developed as a government housing complex. They argued that 15 hectares in their village of Sunter in North Jakarta were taken over by the government in 1983 to build a housing complex, part of which (7 hectares) consisted of the house plots in the *kampung*. In this particular case the mayor of North Jakarta admitted that many of the former residents did have the right to own these areas (*Jakarta Post*, December 8, 1984).

**Rural Land Ownership Disputes in Rural Areas.** Land disputes are still a major feature of village life in Indonesia. One interesting case that came up in 1984 (*Indonesian Times*, March 19, 1984) reflected the changes in local government and the effect of these changes on the traditional allocation of land in villages, all of which caused a confusing situation. In this case hundreds of residents in the area of Bekasi, West Java, found that 155 hectares of *sawah* they had tilled over many years was suddenly taken over by the Bekasi district government. This was *bengkok* land, which is given to village officials as a source of income. The officials concerned had handed the rights of this land to 130 residents in this village to till and had received back a percentage of the crops after the harvest. Unfortunately, when many of these villages were raised to subdistricts, the village leaders were given salaries by the government and lost their rights to the *bengkok* land. This land was then handed over to the district-level government that allocated the land for construction and offered compensation to the resident tillers. As usual in these cases, the compensation offered was very low, about Rp15 per square kilometer, compared to the value of the land, which was estimated at Rp3,000 per square kilometer. Thus, a lawsuit ensued.

Changes in status, in residency, and in population, including the internal movement of people in Indonesia as it developed in the 1970s, led to rapidly changing conditions and increasing problems in land matters at the village level. This case well illustrates that with the development of the country, many of the traditional arrangements were rapidly disappearing, a situation that created confusion and an increasing number of land-related disputes.

## Land Taxation

A major aspect of land policy in this period was the role played by land tax in the attempts to help the development of both the rural and the urban areas and to generate income for the country's economy. Land tax in Indonesia has historically been one of the main tax instruments, and its importance took on added significance in the late 1970s. During this time an attempt was made to increase the nonoil revenue contribution of the country's total tax revenues to lessen the country's dependence on oil because of the fluctuation in world prices and the forecast of rapidly diminishing supplies of oil by the late twentieth century.

In Indonesia the balance of the revenues at the provincial level usually comes from central government sources with only a small percentage being generated from the local level. Thus, in the 1980/1981 period, 72.8 percent of provincial revenue was derived from central government grants and only 12.8 percent from local taxes (Table 3.2). Local taxes are raised from motor vehicles, hotels, restaurants, and the IPEDA land tax. These were mainly raised in urban areas because these areas in Indonesia raise far more revenue per head than the rural areas, with a ratio of around 6 to 1 (World Bank 1984, p. 160). Local revenues have not grown in any significant way under the New Order: Receipts are running at a rate below the growth rate of the economy as a whole in the 1970s and early 1980s. This situation, with the predominance of oil revenue that is so susceptible to world price fluctuation yet in the 1980s was still contributing 67 percent of Indonesia's national budget, was of major concern to the government of Indonesia, which by the early 1980s was actively seeking ways of redressing this imbalance.

The land and property taxes in Indonesia consist of three taxes that correspond to the three main levels of government. At the central government level is the net wealth tax (the *Pajah Pendapatan Kekayaan* or PPK) that accrues to the central government; at the provincial level is the household tax (*pajak rumah tangga*); and at the urban/district level is the IPEDA land tax. There are considerable overlap among these

**Table 3.2.**
**Sources of Provincial Revenue**
(*percent contribution by source*)

| Source of Finance | 1972–1977 | 1978–1979 | 1980–1981 |
|---|---|---|---|
| Central government grant | 67.4 | 69.8 | 72.8 |
| Local taxes and charges | 13.2 | 12.7 | 12.8 |
| Loans | 1.0 | 1.6 | 0.8 |
| Others[a] | 18.4 | 15.9 | 13.6 |
| Total | 100.0 | 100.0 | 100.0 |

*Source:* Department of Finance, Jakarta (1982).
[a] Includes revenues from locally owned public enterprises, cesses on forestry products and cloves, and miscellaneous income and miscategorized funds from other sources. The large size of this other category partly reflects a lack of uniformity in accounting practices.

three taxes and potential for improved coordination and consolidation. The wealth tax, for instance, is not productive. Experience in other countries suggests that on average it is reasonable to raise total revenues from wealth taxes in the range of 1 to 1.5 percent of total wealth, while in Indonesia collections in the 1970s averaged about one-tenth this level. The provincial household tax, which is not collected in all provinces, is particularly ineffective and complex. It is levied on the assessed annual rental of houses (5 percent), motor vehicles (5 percent), and the value of furniture (2 percent). Different teams collect revenue for the household tax and the IPEDA tax from the same households and from the same tax base. These groups do not share records and there is apparently very little coordination.

Of these taxes the IPEDA land tax is by far the most widely collected direct tax in Indonesia. It is regarded as a people's tax since it represents an opportunity for everyone to make a contribution, however small, to the development effort in the region. The IPEDA tax has its roots in Indonesia's colonial past, starting with a land rent and its assignment under Raffles and continuing with various modifications in the Dutch colonial period when the first individual rural property tax, the *verpanding*, was introduced. At Indonesia's independence the land tax system that had evolved under the colonial system and that by the time of independence had achieved considerable sophistication in Java, Bali, Lombok, and South Sulawesi in its assessment and collection was too closely associated with the colonial past to retain (Booth 1981, p. 46). Thus, the land tax as such was abolished and replaced by an agriculture income tax. This new agriculture tax proved to be unsatisfactory, so in 1959 the concept of land taxation was revised with a new tax (*pajak hasil bumi*) on land yields. One important aspect of this change was that the tax was now to be used as a source of income for the district as against the central government to spend on rural development projects. In 1965 the name *pajak hasil bumi* was changed to IPEDA, linking in the name to local development as the farmer was not seen as now paying just a land tax but also making a contribution to local and, by implication, to his or her own development (Booth 1981, p. 47).

The IPEDA tax was initially applied to the rural areas and then extended in 1967 with a major reorganization of its scope and adminis- tration. It now consists of two broad categories of land taxes: property taxes (for urban and rural households, businesses, and farms) and land taxes (relating to yields from mining, forestry, and plantations).[6] For each of these sectors IPEDA is in theory a 5 percent tax on actual or potential revenue from the land use. IPEDA is a central government tax that is listed in the national budget and entered in the local and regional budgets under the heading of central subsidies. Its administra- tion comes under the Directorate General of Finance within the central government Ministry of Finance, which has regional branch offices staffed by central government civil servants responsible for the tax's collection.[7] For the property taxes, annual assessments are prepared by the IPEDA officers who in the late 1970s totaled over 3,000 officials. A 10 percent collection fee is then paid to teams of thousands of local regional part-time collectors who collect the tax from the estimated 30 million registered taxpayers who are liable to pay the IPEDA tax. Of this total, 3.5 million are located in the major urban centers and the balance in the rural areas (World Bank 1984, pp. 162–163). The districts and small towns or second-level regions receive the largest share of total IPEDA tax revenues. The IPEDA tax provides 10 percent of Indonesia's total nonoil revenues, or 3 percent of the total tax revenues in the country.

Although the major part, 85 percent of IPEDA's total revenue comes from the rural areas, it is not a particularly effective tax at this level because many of the rural farmers are near the poverty level. In the urban areas it has far greater potential although that potential is usually underestimated. Given the very rapid increase of both land values and rentals in major urban areas since 1970, urban land in Indonesia is greatly under taxed (Booth 1981, p. 130). If the rural IPEDA is not very effective, however, it does contribute 70 to 90 percent of the total revenue of the districts as opposed to only 2 to 4 percent in the cities (Lerche 1976, p. 34).

Unlike many other methods of taxation, the IPEDA Tax system does not provide many loopholes for evasion, but its collection, even with the 10 percent compensation going to the collectors, tends to be slow, with 50 to 60 percent of the assessment being collected in the year of assessment and another 20 to 25 percent in subsequent years. The overall collection ratio is 70 to 80 percent (World Bank 1974, p. 163). Collection rates, however, vary considerably by type of property, with first-year receipts for poor residential urban areas often only 30 to 40 percent of the assessed value but over 80 percent for commercial properties. Administrative costs are high: They total about 20 percent of the tax collected because of the 10 percent paid to the collectors and an estimated 10 percent for other costs. As a system it needs rationalization since a large percentage of the rural landowners pays assessments as low as $1 a year, which is noneconomic in terms of balancing the administrative costs (Lerche 1976, p. 320). The majority of urban taxpayers currently contributes very little revenue, and about one-third of all taxpayers fail to cover the average cost, estimated at Rp2,000 (US$3) per assessment, of collection.[8] The average assessment, for instance, in Jakarta in 1982 was Rp14,000 (US$23) but 50 percent of all taxpayers were assessed at less than Rp5,000 (US$8) implying collections of less than Rp3,500 (US$6). For other major cities average assessments are about half the level in Jakarta. Only a few households are assessed in the middle- and upper-income categories. In Surabaya, for example, only 7 percent of households were required to pay taxes of more than Rp15,000 in 1982, although Surabaya has much middle-class housing and is one of the richest cities in the country.

Urban IPEDA consists of a 5 percent tax on the imputed rental value of the land, with the annual rental value calculated as 6 percent and 3 percent of the assessed value of commercial and residential land respectively. The assessed value in turn is 60 percent of estimated market value so the effective tax is designed to be 0.18 percent of market value for commercial land and 0.09 percent of market value for residential land. Buildings on the land are taxed at a slightly lower rate. Market value of land and property per $m^2$ are not estimated on an individual plot basis but according to the street or zone in which the property is located. The present system derives from a 1978 decree that introduced a market-value-based system of assessment. Land values were to be updated by survey every 3 years and although this has not happened, there was a sharp increase in assessments, raised by an average of about 40 percent in May 1982. For commercial properties, rates now range from Rp1.3 to Rp504 per $m^2$ for land and Rp19.6 to Rp352 per $m^2$ for buildings; for residential properties, rates are half these amounts (World Bank 1985, p. 103).

IPEDA taxation in urban areas is particularly important in modern Indonesia because it is the key element in providing funding for the development of the country's rapidly growing cities as well as having the greatest potential for increasing overall revenue. Local assessments are made by the IPEDA offices, and while these have been revised in 1978 and 1982, they do not reflect the rapidly increasing urban values in the major cities. The IPEDA contribution to Jakarta's budget, for instance, the largest city in Indonesia, is between only 2.5 and 4 percent of the city's budget; in Surabaya, the second largest urban area, it is only 2 percent; and reflecting the lack of other tax sources, it is no more than 10 percent in the smaller cities.

Although clearly more realistic assessments are needed, the IPEDA remains the most important single tax source for cities in Indonesia, with the one exception of Jakarta where other local taxes are greater (Lerche 1976, p. 326).[9] However, IPEDA revenues should be far greater since in Indonesia, like in many countries, the major sources of the nation's wealth accumulate in the cities so that only a minor part of the nation's wealth is received by the IPEDA. This need to maximize the effectiveness of the IPEDA land tax is vividly illustrated when one compares the contribution of the land tax revenue of Jakarta with other major world cities. Thus, the 2.5 to 4 percent obtained from land tax in Jakarta is very low in comparison with Manila (14 percent), Mexico City (20 percent), or Calcutta (57 percent).

An examination of the present weaknesses in the system as it is applied to the urban areas shows that very little allowance is made for the increased value of private properties in the cities. This situation applies particularly to high-value buildings such as international hotels and bank buildings that are clearly undertaxed because of the lack of an individual appraisal method. One study (Lerche 1976) has shown that there is a great scope for improving the land tax in Jakarta and other urban areas with an estimated gap of $5 million between the present IPEDA assessment and the potential revenue. Improvements could be made also in the administration. It is estimated that 15 to 20 percent of properties escape taxation by not being registered by the IPEDA or not being fully assessed; IPEDA authorities rely on information about property size and improvements provided by the taxpayer, and those data are very rarely checked. Late payments are common and, with the high inflation existing in Indonesia, revenues are affected. After allowing for collection of commissions and costs, it has been estimated that the present IPEDA may not even reach 50 percent of the assessment potential without a thorough revision of the present system.

The urban IPEDA can clearly be improved in a number of areas. These include a change in the system that allows changes in the underlying index assessment that cumulatively remains at 5 percent of rental value as set by the BAL and that is uniformly applied to all types of properties. A number of studies (Oldman and Holland 1972; Lerche 1976) have explored the scope for increased property tax rates and increased collection efficiency. In addition to raising the basic 5 percent rate on the assessed rental value, these studies have recommended raising the ratio of assessed value to market value (currently 60 percent), raising the ratio of rental value to assessed value (currently 6 percent), fully taxing residential property (instead of the current 50 percent exemption), abolishing the ceiling on assessed property values (which results in undertaxation of high-value commercial property), and reviewing market land data more frequently since IPEDA assessments do not usually keep pace with rising land values, particularly in high-value and improved areas. In 1985 consideration was being given to adopting a number of changes on a pilot basis in Surabaya following a study (Jeffries 1980) that recommended the adoption of a new assessment system based on market valuation of individual properties rather than on the present classification system. The valuation system would be based on an analysis of sales data to establish land and building values. Improved mapping techniques would be introduced, and site data would be computerized. Central business district properties would be professionally appraised, and a major effort would be made to improve land registration and monitor changes of ownership.

A second area is the need for clearer legal sanctions to enforce payment. Presently a 5 percent fine is added but rarely collected on late payments, and other sanctions, such as the seizing of property, although theoretically possible, have never been applied. More incentives could also be built in at the local government level to aid IPEDA collection. The central government currently sets collection targets on a yearly basis, usually at 80 percent of the total assessments plus 50 percent of arrears. These targets are easy to meet, and once they are met, there is no incentive for local authorities to try to exceed the imposed target.

A third area that needs improvement is the collection system. Overall collection costs are some 15 to 20 percent of the gross collections in Jakarta. One problem is that the IPEDA collection applies to all properties. Thus, of about 300,000 properties assessed in 1973, 50 percent of those that involved a tax liability were valued at only US$1. By improving assessments and by bringing the effective tax rate up to the legal limit, it has been calculated that collections would increase more than fivefold, and thus, average collection costs per taxpayer would be cut by half (Lerche 1976). If the limited administrative resources, especially qualified personnel, concentrated more on high-value private and commercial properties, revenues clearly could be increased considerably at little extra cost.

Finally we should reemphasize that the current rates of land and property taxation in Indonesia are low by any international standards. In many countries the effective rate of taxation is about 1 percent of the market value of property rather than the 0.1 percent in Indonesia.[10] A tenfold increase in the effective tax rate for the IPEDA, whether on urban or rural land, would require a major sustained effort but would not be an unreasonable target by the end of the Fifth Five-Year Plan (1994/1995). By the early 1990s receipts from the urban IPEDA (Rp21 billion in 1981/1982) could, it is suggested (World Bank 1984, p. 168), finance about a third of all new investments in urban services and could almost single-handedly compensate for any declining contribution from the central government. Higher effective tax rates may also bring some subsidiary benefits such as restraining the growth in land prices, encouraging investment, and discouraging speculation in idle land (Shoup 1983).

Land property tax, whether on urban or rural land, is a sensitive political issue in Indonesia because it is historically linked to land taxation and the country's earlier exploitation under colonial rule. It is also a tax that traditionally has been focused mainly on the rural areas. Yet IPEDA does offer an important resource to meet the growing revenue needs—particularly those of Indonesia's growing cities—and in evolving an effective national land policy, it is clearly a crucial area to be addressed.

## Land Reform

As noted earlier, although land reform was not given major policy emphasis in the New Order period, the land reform program introduced with the BAL in the 1960s continued to be implemented at the administrative level. Programs such as PRONA for accelerated land registration were introduced to speed up the process of land distribution. Unfortunately, while the PRONA program attempted to certify as much land as possible, the slow and cumbersome bureaucracy with the high costs in terms of the illegal levies attached to every step in the registration process led to lengthy delays and seriously undercut the program. Absentee landownership in the early 1980s remained a major and growing problem. A report by the Department of Home Affairs in 1984 noted that tens of thousands of hectares of land had been identified as belonging to absentee landlords and that steps were being taken to revoke rights of the owners (*Kompas*, July 8, 1984). The report pointed out that the owners of land who were living outside these areas often tried to cover their absence by, for example, planting a number of cassava plants on the land. This kind of problem led to a meeting between the president and the minister of home affairs in 1984 that led to the instruction that the government should push forward with settling outstanding land problems. It is interesting to note, however, that the emphasis was placed on the fact that these land problems were holding up development projects, particularly infrastructure projects, and that it was in this context, rather than that of land reform, that they had to be addressed.

One can see the focus of land policy in the 1980s moving from that of land redistribution of the early 1960s to the need to solve land problems that were hindering the effective implementation of government development policies. At the same time there is government pressure to reduce the number of small farmers who owned less than 0.5 hectare of land. The government argued that the small land plots were not economical and were one of the main causes of rural impoverishment. The fact that these small farmers had declined in number from 11 million in 1980 to 8.7 million in 1983 was seen by the government as a sign of progress. To reduce this number to an estimated 4.5 million by 1989, the minister of agriculture noted that while there would be no compulsion, the government would encourage them to sell their land (*Kompas*, February 9, 1984). Various alternatives were offered to farmers who were willing to sell their land, including training programs to increase their skills for plantation work or for the transmigration program. No reference is made to large landholdings or the possibility that there would be inequality in terms of landownership. Again, this government statement reflected the thinking in the New Order period that land and its value were seen in the context of the government's overall development program, which placed prime emphasis on development rather than on the need for social equity.

Another feature of the land reform era of the 1960s was the consideration for compensation of confiscated land. Compensation was again considered in the early 1980s. In 1983 an interesting case came up in which three former sultans of Cirebon filed a lawsuit for the restoration of their land that had been appropriated following the enforcement of the BAL (*Kompas*, November 12, 1984). These three sultans had given up the major part of their land (ranging from 1,200 to 1,600 hectares) and had received 20 hectares for agricultural development and 5 hectares for their palaces. This land had been distributed for local needs including land for a mosque, local government buildings, a marketplace, and bus terminals. In the lawsuit the sultans requested the restoration of their land to what it was before land reform, claiming that it was inherited land that had been in their families for generations. They pointed out that they had not been paid compensation and thus could not live on the revenue from the land cut down as it was to the small areas in light of their commitments to keep their palaces open and their staffs employed. Thus, 23 years after land reform was introduced in Indonesia, this case showed clearly that there were instances, and not just isolated ones, where land had not been compensated for. In hindsight, one can see that after the first very active years of land reform after the passing of the BAL in 1960, new and more urgent political and economic imperatives had virtually brought the program to a halt from the early 1970s onward and a great deal of the implementation was left to be carried out.

## Conclusion

Although there were continuing problems relating to land and land issues in the 1970s and early 1980s, improvements tended to be ad hoc and were stimulated when they did occur by more general economic factors. There was no attempt to revise or improve the BAL of the early 1960s and no formulation of general land policy guidelines. Land reform, which had been such a prominent feature of the 1960s, became in the 1980s almost a dead issue due to its lack of immediate importance and to the emphasis on the what were seen as more important government policies. Yet the rapid development of the country both on and off Java, with major sectoral changes in the rural areas as well as rapid urbanization, resulted in a growing number of land-related issues that needed to be addressed. Thus, as Indonesia moved into the mid 1980s, the need for a comprehensive national land policy that provided adequate legislation, allied with the means to back up its implementation, was becoming more imperative.

## Notes

1. Bimas is an acronym that stands for *bimbingan massal*, an agricultural intensification program for rice and other crops. Since the mid-1960s most of the government rice intensification programs have been referred to by this name. Inmas (Intensifikasi Massal) is an agriculture extension program for rice and other food crops. It does not, unlike Bimas, provide credit to participants but supplies them with subsidized inputs.

2. Village *bengkok* land is given to village officials who have the right to work it and collect the product as long as they retain their official position. A World Bank survey found that 34 percent of the village head's income in Java came from *bengkok* land. The average size of land allotments associated with the village head's position was 6 hectares in one *kabupaten* surveyed, which even if not all *sawah*, is a large holding in Java (see World Bank 1974, vol. 3, Annex 4, pp. 4–5).
3. The 1983 census had not been fully published and analyzed at the time of writing. See Indonesia, Bureau of Statistics (1963, 1973).
4. The 1973 census did not directly address the problems of tenancy and landholdings but concentrated on the structure of land used for cropping patterns, the quality of irrigation, the use of new imports such as fertilizers and pesticides, and the extent of livestock holdings.
5. The survey was carried out between January and July 1985 of the Jakarta English-language newspapers (*Jakarta Post, Indonesian Times,* and *Indonesian Observer*) and the main Jakarta Indonesian-language dailies (*Kompas, Sinar Harapan,* and *Merdeka*).
6. The latter taxes (known as "sector PIII") are very much less broadly based than the urban and rural property taxes.
7. For the forests and plantation taxes, revenues are collected by a special IPEDA inspectorate directly under the Department of Finance rather than as for rural and urban IPEDA, which is collected by agents of the local governments.
8. Data on collection costs are not available in any detail. However if the 10 percent collection fee is added to the 11 percent overhead charge announced for IPEDA in 1981, the average collection charges were over Rp2000 per assessment in 1981 (World Bank 1984, p. 166).
9. Jakarta is the exception because the main part of its taxes comes from other tax bases. Thus, in 1973 the main taxes were derived from the motor vehicle tax (37 percent), automobile transport tax (11.4 percent), and entertainment tax (9.45 percent) with IPEDA contributing only 4.3 percent (Lerche 1976, pp. 320–323).
10. For example, in Taiwan the land value tax is graduated from 1.5 percent to 7 percent of assessed value and in Jamaica, from 1 to 4.5 percent.

# 4

# A National Land Policy
# for the 1980s

Indonesia has not in the past seen any form of comprehensive national land policy, but it faces the need today to establish just such a policy to provide it with a sounder basis for sustaining its present development. Such a policy would provide a clear set of guidelines applicable at all levels of Indonesian life and backed up by the legal enactments and the mechanisms for its implementation to cover all aspects of land affairs in modern Indonesia. The policy would be given strong bureaucratic and political backing so that it can be fully effective in dealing in a comprehensive way with the wide array of land issues facing Indonesia. It would incorporate many of the elements of the BAL of 1960 and later enactments but would revise, strengthen, and add to these to remedy both previous weaknesses and to take into account the considerable changes in Indonesia in recent years.

A number of factors must be taken into account in the formulation of such a comprehensive national land policy for Indonesia in the 1980s. One is the recognition of the continuing importance of land in Indonesia due to the country's predominantly agricultural nature. Land is still, for all the modern developments in the country, the basis for the subsistence of 57 percent of the population; it provides the majority of the agricultural commodities that form 61 percent of the nonoil exports (World Bank 1985, p. 20); and it is still the prime target of investment from the villager to the richer city dweller. A second factor is the continuing role of land in the sociopolitical framework of Indonesian society. Discontent over land and land problems historically has given rise to political unrest, and that possibility remains alive today. Indonesia under the New Order has seen the longest period of stability since its independence, but its present unity was not easily reached given the enormous diversity of the country, the existence of the country's numerous ethnic groups with their own traditions and *adat* laws, and the long history in early postindependence Indonesia of regional rebellions and unrest. This stability, however, could still easily be disrupted. Thus, all aspects of land affairs and land problems are key elements in the makeup of modern Indonesian society. If land problems arise and are not adequately dealt with, they can and will cause unrest, and thus their resolution is of continuing importance to the well-being of Indonesian society.

A third factor is the rapid development of Indonesia since the 1960s and, just as important, the priorities of that development. Rapid development has brought about vast changes in Indonesian rural as well as urban society that have resulted in marked changes in the structure of rural society as well as the growing urbanization of the country. At the same time, the New Order government that came to power in 1965/1966 focused its policies on what it saw as the most important priority, the rapid economic development of the country. In this process the importance of social equity, which was a prominent concern in the country's early postindependence years, was not entirely lost but came to be seen more as a matter of providing adequate incomes and assistance to Indonesia's population as a whole rather than one of just the redistribution of land. Consequently, land reform, which was a major policy concern under the Old Order and was seen as being one of the main instruments in bringing about greater equality, has not been given similar importance under the New Order government.

Given these factors, a main policy priority in present-day Indonesia is for a comprehensive national land policy that can provide a clear set of guidelines to support the development of the country. Such a policy should fit the present pattern of landownership and use in Indonesia and address land reform issues where they still exist as well as the more general and growing urgent problems of land administration in what is a rapidly modernizing and changing society. This chapter examines the makeup of such a policy, the main issues to be addressed, the general framework for such a policy, and finally, the specific components that need to be included.

## Components of National Land Policy

### General Guidelines

It is important that a national land policy for the 1980s address many of the long-term problems that still exist in the present-day ownership and distribution of land. Thus, it must address the continuing clash between modern and *adat* systems of land law that in many areas remain unclear or are a matter of dispute. The land policy must also rationalize the present land legislation, including the BAL, and provide what additional legislation is required to establish a comprehensive policy that is applicable to all parts of the country and to all levels of the society. Such a policy must cover the enormous changes in Indonesia including changes in farming patterns as well as social changes that have taken place since the New Order came to power in 1965/1966. All these factors have engendered new types of land problems and will engender many more as these kinds of changes continue in Indonesia over the next decades. At a more microlevel, the new national land policy must address clearly and effectively the problems of land distribution, land registration, and land rights at all levels of the society. Above all, any national policy must be an agreed on and enforceable policy with the full commitment to it of the government and its resources aided by the country's legal system.

Looking in more detailed terms of what is needed, some of the necessary legislation already exists on the Indonesian statute book. The BAL and other enactments of the 1960s laid down a system for landholdings that provides a general basis to underpin a present national policy. That legislation allowed for the integration of Western civil law concepts with the existing *adat* and covered land taxes, landholdings, and ownership systems. It also provided the means for converting titles issued under prior titling systems with the types of rights now provided by the BAL. It clarified and defined clearly the role of land in Indonesia's social and economic state *Pancasila* system and laid out a system of land registration that provided a level of legal security to ensure equity in landholdings and ownership. In hindsight it set up a system at the right time in Indonesia's development that limited large landholdings, tried to rationalize redistribution, instituted land registration with certificates that brought in a public record of transfer of ownership and encumbrances, and gave the government some of the tools to control land use at the time when the country was moving into a take-off stage of development.

The BAL had a number of weaknesses that undermined its effectiveness. The limits placed on landholdings of 2 to 20 hectares were not realistic and have needed revision since the 1960s. Many of its general provisions, while providing the general legal institutional framework for the legal requirements and rights of landownership in Indonesia, needed additional legislation to make them fully effective. In particular, the fact that it did not impose compulsory land registration and certification or fully secure an individual's land rights were major weaknesses. One can see that the BAL was an appropriate first step in the process of setting up a national land system in the 1960s but one that was not followed up adequately in subsequent years. By the late 1970s even the basic enactments were in need of considerable alteration so they would fit into the modern Indonesia that was rapidly emerging. The specific components of a national land policy can be divided into immediate steps that need to be taken within the framework of existing legislation and practice and a number of long-term improvements that together would provide a coherent and fully comprehensive national land policy.

*Immediate Steps*

**Compulsory Land Registration.** Legislation is required to make land registration and certification compulsory in all land transactions. This would back up strongly the land registration procedures already laid down under the BAL. Two mechanisms in particular could be used to enforce compulsory legislation. One would be to require compulsory registration as part of all land transactions. A second would be to link compulsory registration with the existing government-supported credit programs. Evidence of land rights currently is required only in a limited number of credit programs and then only on an irregular basis. These requirements could well be tightened up to make evidence of land rights and thus land registration a basic requirement for borrowing under any government credit scheme (see Appendix B for details).

**Readjustment of the Present Limits of Landownership.** The current limits of ownership date back to the BAL of 1960 and need to be related more closely to the wide variation of landholdings and different types of land uses in Indonesia as well as changes in the rural areas in recent years. The landholding ceiling established under the BAL varied according to the population density. Thus, in Java, for example, the ceiling was established at 5 hectares of *sawah* and 6 hectares of dry land and up to 15 hectares of *sawah* and 20 hectares of dry land in the less thickly populated areas of the country outside Java. With 82 percent of the farmers in Java and 71 percent of farmers throughout Indonesia having holdings of one hectare or less and no more than 2 percent throughout the country owning more than 5 hectares, these ceilings are far too high (See Table 1.5). Apart from not being generally applicable, they also leave far too little land to be reallocated. Thus, new and reduced ceilings need to be established so land redistribution can be implemented effectively. A revised ceiling for Java could well be half the present ceiling.

**Absentee Ownership.** A tightening and revision of the legislation regarding absentee ownership is needed. Two problems are associated with this phenomenon. First, Article 10 of the BAL is unclear as to what exactly constitutes absentee ownership. Second, the growth of the country, particularly with the recent increase in urbanization, has led to a significant growth in absentee ownership, and this needs to be halted.

*Long-term Improvements*

A number of long-term improvements are needed to strengthen and improve the present system of land administration and make it more responsive to present-day needs. These include both legislative changes and organizational improvements.

**Legislative Changes.** The existing legislation pertaining to land needs thorough revision because the present legislation is often confusing and sometimes conflicting. Since the enactment of the BAL in 1960, a large number of regulations regarding land have been made that cover a variety of aspects. What is needed now is a review and evaluation of these regulations to ensure that they provide a comprehensive and coherent set of legislative requirements. One study, for instance, showed that Agrarian Affairs staff and others dealing with land matters at various levels of government in the early 1980s had little under-standing of the contents of the various regulations in current use and what they encompassed (USAID 1982). What is needed now is clarification of existing regulations, deletion of a number of items, language modification, and consolidation of the various enactments into one comprehensive set of legal and administrative requirements. Amendments to the current legislation are urgently required in three specific areas.

*Strengthening of the Role of the Modern National System of Law in Relation to* Adat *Law.* Although the BAL (Article 3) placed the *adat* under the modern legal system, the still strong hold of traditional *adat* in many parts of the country is a considerable hindrance to development. One major example is the inability of the government to develop unused agricultural land in the outer islands because of *adat* claims (Ross 1984, p. 33).

*Legislation to Enable Speedier Land Acquisition Procedures.* All areas of the country—in particular, Java—still suffer from the lack of a speedy appropriation of land required for public purposes. By the early 1980s delays in land registration were seriously holding up government development programs at all levels and were highlighted by the World Bank (1985, p. 24) as one of the main constraints in project implementation. Part of this is due to the difficulties in putting the existing legislation into effect. The first enactment in this area, the Expropriation Law (Law No. 20, 1961), requires presidential authority and is seldom used. Its successor, the Regulation of the Minister of Home Affairs (No. 15, 1975), requires the consent of all parties involved and cannot be effectively implemented without that consent. In practice, the need for compromise in such cases leads to a substantial increase in the amount of compensation that must be paid since there is no mechanism for forcing acceptance of compensation set by the committee based on the market price for land. There is also no mechanism for review by a third party or court of the amount of compensation to be paid.

In the short term, Regulation No. 15 of 1975 needs to be strengthened to provide a more effective set of procedures for discussion and resolution in such cases and a more precise standard to calculate the amount of compensation to be paid. In addition, the local agencies requesting land acquisition should be allowed and even required to do much of the necessary surveying and mapping for the local Agraria office since this would save the present considerable delays that are caused by Agraria's lack of skilled staff. Agraria would then issue the necessary certificates. With regard to a standard of compensation, the market price should be more specifically defined as the price of recent land sales by similarly placed sellers. A basic price should be set at regular 6 month or 1 year intervals for cases where there were no recent sales for comparison to determine compensation.

In the long term the Basic Expropriation Law No. 20 of 1961 should be amended to permit the mayor or district head in most cases to carry out expropriation, to define the amount of compensation to be paid as the market price for land at that locality at that point in time, and to allow the adoption of more precise procedures of conflict resolution between the parties prior to the instigation of the formal expropriation process.

*Review of Foreign Ownership Limitations.* One of the major constraints to economic development in Indonesia today is the present limits on foreign ownership or use of land by non-Indonesians. These limits include a ban on foreign land tenure and a 30 year limit on agrarian land-use permits issued to non-Indonesians. These "bedrock" policies, as an Indonesian government spokesman termed them (Kaye 1985), are creating serious constraints in terms of attracting much-needed foreign investment, particularly into the Indonesian agriculture sector.

Thus, review and modification of the present legislation in this area are necessary.

**Organizational Improvements.** Major organizational improvements in the existing land administration system are urgently needed. This system quite rightly has been noted as being cumbersome in its administrative procedures (World Bank 1985, p. 24) and needs considerable stream-lining. The most immediate improvements are needed in two main areas, those of land registration and land administration, including the provision of more Agraria offices in the rural areas as well as additional staffing and training.

*Land Registration.* An immediate need is to establish priority areas for land registration. Currently only a very limited number of areas that come under major government projects such as the nucleus estate smallholder program (NES) are adequately mapped. A very low percentage of land is titled, and throughout the country there are a very large number of small individual parcels of land and also a large number of individual owners. Given the size of Indonesia with the limited resources to carry out nationwide registration, it has been estimated that even an accelerated land registration program could take 100 years to implement (USAID 1982). Thus, prioritization of key areas for land registration is an urgent priority. Some attempts to do this have been already started with the introduction in the 1970s of special government agriculture development programs in the rural areas. In urban areas the guided-land-development (GLD) type of scheme that is being used in the Jabotabek Project around Jakarta provides an example of an innovative approach to prioritization and a model for the utilization of private land on the outskirts of Indonesia's growing urban areas for public develop-ment (World Bank 1984, p. 94). However, while these programs are individually beneficial, there is no countrywide attempt to set up a system of priorities in land surveying, mapping, or regulation that would provide a sound basis for national development in the future.

Even if land registration were made compulsory, there clearly would still be a number of impediments in present-day Indonesia to its full acceptance. One of these is the stronghold of *adat* in many parts of the country, which is not surprising in light of the centuries of *adat* practice compared to the 25 years or so the modern system initially established under the BAL. In addition, there are problems of communication, including the lack of physical access to Agraria offices, that still apply to many parts of Indonesia today due to the sheer size of the country. Many villages are located a considerable distance from the district office, and the rural landowner is often isolated and does not have the time or money to travel to the district agrarian office to file an application. There is also a lack of understanding by landowners as to what forms to file and how to fill them out, what fees to pay, what Agraria offices to contact, and what supporting documents are required. These problems arise mainly with the small landowners; the larger landowners are usually well educated, have comparatively large holdings, and are relatively wealthy. If they do not understand the procedures, they can hire a middleperson to guide them through the Agraria bureaucracy. However, the greater number of farmers is in the small landowners class, and they need help to understand the system and the benefits of registration. Large-scale publicity is needed to provide such help by the government so that there is adequate knowledge of land registration procedures, whether urban or rural; the process of obtaining land certificates; the costs involved; and the benefits that flow from obtaining certificates.

Expanding landowners' knowledge could be accomplished in a number of ways. One way is to extend the present network of Agraria offices down to the subdistrict and perhaps village level and to provide more trained staff. A second is to use an office on wheels approach with mobile Agraria offices located in the villages. The office on wheels approach also has other benefits: These village-level offices can help identify excess landholdings and absentee ownership in the individual village areas. In addition, as PRONA has shown on a small scale that could certainly work on a larger scale, booklets, posters, and other media methods could be used to sell the advantages of land registration.

Modification of the present system of forms and certification required in the registration application process is urgently needed. An applicant for land currently has to fill out up to six forms depending on the type of registration. The overall paperwork involved in land registration and in land administration is overcumbersome and needs rationalization.

There is a need to revise fees in some areas. Studies of government projects such as the NES, rice land conversion (*Percetakan Sawah*), and other land development schemes where the individuals are charged the full cost of registration show that the participants feel that the fees are reasonable, especially since they can pay in small annual installments (USAID 1982). However, the fees charged in other cases need reappraisal. One example is the fee paid to the land deed official for land transfers. This is an arbitrary fee, being 1.5 percent of the market value of the land and often results in unfair, inequitable, and ambiguous charges. Consequently, a flat rate needs to be established for land transfers. There is also currently no difference in the fees charged to rich or poor landowners, illustrating the need for a graduated fee system in which fees for surveying and mapping are charged on the size of the landholdings and the class of the land.[1]

One way to make fees equitable would be to utilize the existing IPEDA (land tax) system of land classification that would ensure that the fees for surveying and mapping a parcel of highly productive land would be more than for a small parcel of dry land. Costs would also be waived for those who could not afford to pay.[2] The use of the IPEDA system has a number of advantages. It has already been developed and has been in operation for many years; it is constantly being expanded to new areas; and it is largely understood by rural landowners. It provides for the costs of surveying and mapping to be allocated on the basis of the relative value of services received. Since a landowner with a large parcel of high-value land receives more benefits from surveying and mapping than one with a small low-value parcel under this system, landowners with large high-value parcels would, if the level of fees were prorated, in effect finance the surveying and mapping of landowners with small low-value parcels.

A land data system is urgently needed to provide accurate and comprehensive statistics on all aspects of land, particularly ownership and registration. In the case of registration there is currently no consistent or uniform manner for collecting national data on registration. Data are usually collected manually, on a case-by-case basis, and are not collated throughout the country. There is also no easy way of retrieving present data stored manually in land offices on cards. This makes any attempt to improve the system difficult, particularly in trying to meet the present increase in demands for registration throughout the country, let alone the increase anticipated with compulsory registration.

There is also a need for more accurate statistical data on land ownership in Indonesia. For instance, a great deal of speculation occurs on what the trend is in average size of landholdings, the extent of absentee landowners, and the rate at which households are becoming landless. The 1963 and 1973 agricultural censuses (Indonesia, Bureau of Statistics) did not record patterns of landownerships or levels of landlessness and covered only households with some access to land (owner, tenant, or other use right) who also cultivated some of the land with their own labor or as managers. Thus, building up an accurate and comprehensive database for land information is of immediate priority. This can be started by introducing a landownership data system using small computers to provide data on trends in size of parcels and hectares per landowner, the extent to which households are selling all their land, and present ownership of those purchasing the land. This kind of database has wider applicability and could provide data for government development programs as well as an ongoing land database to backup and amend census data.

*Land Administration.* One crucial component of a national land policy is an effective land administration system. The current organizational structure for land administration to some extent is adequate, providing both a strong bureaucratic base in the Department of Home Affairs and having offices at the appropriate levels of the local government structure. However, there is a clear need to extend the existing offices down to the subdistrict and village levels to provide wider coverage and easier access in the rural areas. Improvements are also needed in the staffing and the provision of training. Even without taking into account additional staff needed in an expanded system, a considerable increase in personnel is needed to staff the present Agraria offices adequately at the central as well as the local government level. In addition, adequate numbers of technical staff are lacking even to maintain the present workload of land measurement for titling without any of the expansion that is proposed in the future.

Many of those staff members currently engaged in the present land administration structure in Indonesia are inadequately trained (USAID 1982), in both administrative and technical areas. Lack of adequate training is particularly evident in the areas of registration procedures and processing, the adjudication of title rights and claims, and the legal and regulatory provisions of land registration. Thus, training is a high priority in the attempt to streamline the system so it can handle comprehensively the land problems in terms of a single overall system. A sustained and well-organized training program to upgrade the efficiency of existing staff must be established. In view of the need for increased numbers of staff members and better training, whether administrative or technical, the initial selection of personnel should come from the pool of high school and university graduates. Then initial training courses are needed, followed by additional training at different stages of an individuals' career development.

### Financial Resources

A comprehensive national land policy like the one being suggested will need considerable increases in current funding to meet the costs of implementation. This funding will be required for the increased costs of surveying and mapping, additional staff, training, and equipment. The present funding comes out of the central government budget that pays for all land administration activities. This funding will, if the political commitment is made to reform the present system, have to be greatly increased. Additional funding could be raised in two areas: one is from the present land tax (IPEDA) and the other is from an existing special tax (*pajak khusus*). The present IPEDA land tax is the most widely collected direct tax in Indonesia, with some 30 million payees in the urban and rural areas. However, its potential is still not fully realized. The IPEDA rates are low by international standards, being 0.1 percent as opposed to 1 percent of the market value of property. It is estimated that a tenfold increase in the effective tax rate for IPEDA, whether urban or rural, would require a major sustained effort but would not be an unreasonable target. Higher effective tax rates would also bring some subsidiary benefits such as restraining the growth in land prices, encouraging investment, and discouraging speculation in idle land (Shoup 1983).[3]

A number of studies have explored the scope of increased property tax rates and increased collection efficiency (Oldman and Holland 1972; Jeffries 1980), and a number of ways to do this were discussed in Chapter 3. The need for reform is indicated by the lack of collection efficiency in IPEDA and the fact that the majority of taxpayers contribute very little revenue, as probably one third of all taxpayers fail to cover the average cost of collection.[4] During 1985, steps were taken to formulate new legislation that would radically revise the present land tax system. Among the proposals that were discussed were the introduction of a new land tax law that would rationalize the present often confusing and antiquated legislation (that in some instances dates back to the 1920s) and the introduction of a single tax rate to simplify the present complex tax rate system. If these proposals come into effect, the present IPEDA land tax would probably be amalgamated into this new, simplified land tax system.

The second tax whose present levels could be maximized, particularly in urban areas, to support the greater budgetary needs of a revised land administration system is the special tax (*pajak khusus*). This is a betterment tax—in fact, the only betterment tax currently being used in Indonesia—and is applied to urban and rural areas in Jakarta.[5] The legislative basis for the *pajak khusus* is a 1972 regulation permitting city authorities to recover 60 percent of the cost of new and improved infrastructure (including roads, bridges, drainage, water supply, and electricity) in areas designated by the governor (Regional Decree No. 1, March 8, 1972). The *pajak khusus* tax is well designed in principle and can be easily expanded both within Jakarta and to other cities. A number of modifications that could significantly raise collections could be instituted. These would include increased publicity in areas scheduled for betterment and signs to make clear what the tax is, who is responsible for paying, and that no land may be transferred without payment. The tax is currently designed to recover only 60 percent of costs, but this figure could be raised substantially (see Appendix C for details).

Other sources would also have to be found to provide additional funds to support the implementation of a national land policy. Indonesia has a laudable history under the New Order of providing development project money to support major national programs. Land administration in both urban and rural areas is clearly reaching the point at which greater government intervention and budgetary support are more than fully warranted.

## Special Areas

Two areas in particular in terms of setting up a national land policy need special attention: the rapidly growing urban areas in the country and the now very large transmigration areas throughout Indonesia's outer islands. While the general recommendations suggested in this chapter apply to both areas, they also need special measures.

**Urban Areas.** The rapid development of Indonesia in the 1970s and early 1980s has brought about a whole new array of land problems in the country's urban areas. The present legal basis is not adequate for urban planning, land use, and controls.[6] What is needed is legislation to establish preferred locations for housing and for industrial development. In both cases, these locations would be based on the availability of adequate municipal infrastructure and social facilities, with consideration also given to the value of the land for other required purposes—in particular, for agriculture. In the case of industrial development, the nearness of new industry to sources of labor and to other existing industry would be particularly relevant.

Other improvements needed include a more efficient system for development and building permissions. The present regulation regarding the granting of development permissions is basically sound, but decision making needs to be moved down to the district/city level rather than, as in most cases today, being made only by the governor and the provincial directorate of Agraria. There is also a lack of adequate enforcement devices if developers do not follow proper procedures because unfortunately the Minister of Home Affairs Regulation No. 5 of 1974 that governs most development permissions did not contain adequate penalty clauses. Building regulations now in force are also not sufficiently flexible to control construction. The present regulations tend to be very detailed and apply in effect only to construction in middle-class and upper-income areas, and they are based on precise types of performmance standards. What is required is greater flexibility in building standards by area, with minimums set for low-income areas.

Much stronger procedures are required to discourage land speculation and to encourage the more efficient use of land in areas scheduled for development. Rapidly growing urban areas in Indonesia, such as Jabotabek, have suffered from large amounts of land being bought up by wealthy individuals and corporations for development that are usually far from any existing infrastructure. In other cases, the financing for such projects is not available, and the land is not productively used (NUDS 1985). The BAL regulation (Article 17) relating to the size and fragmentation of landholdings is not applied in urban areas. A vacant land tax needs to be introduced to limit both the holding of vacant land or not fully utilized land in urban areas.

Finally, much stronger application of the existing law regarding illegal possession is needed, with the support of effective institutional procedures. In general, Indonesia's urban areas, because of the rapid urbanization of the country, require specific attention and special policy guidelines within the framework of the proposed national land policy.

**Transmigration Areas.** The rapid opening up of land in the other islands due to transmigration, with the very large movement of some 2.5 million people to the new settlement areas in the Third Five-Year Development Plan (1979-1980 to 1983/1984), raises a special set of problems. Transmigrants from Java in 1980 made up an average of 15 percent of the local provincial population throughout Indonesia (World Bank 1985, p. 161).

With the filling up of available areas in Sumatra and Sulawesi, the focus of transmigration is moving, under the Fourth Five-Year Development Plan (1984/1985 to 1988/1989), to Irian Jaya and Kalimantan. In these areas as well as in the existing areas, land problems need particular attention. One major problem is the frequent clash between the new migrants and the local population over land rights. With *adat* usage common in the usually remote and isolated transmigration areas and with inadequate presettlement surveying and land mapping, more care will have to be taken in the future to avoid land conflicts.

On a broader front, transmigration has become so large that it can no longer be seen as a single government program but one that will have enormous impact on all aspects of land administration due to the great number of people who move and the areas developed. New transmigration sites currently come under the Department of Transmigration for the first 5 years and then move to a more regular village status under the Department of Home Affairs. There is presently little coordination between the two departments, and greater coordination will certainly be needed in the future from the beginning of the settlement process so that the now frequent land problems can be minimized.

## Conclusion

A great opportunity currently exists in Indonesia to formulate and implement a comprehensive national land policy and, with it, to improve the existing system of land administration to enable it to meet effectively the increased demands placed on it by the country's development. However, any national land policy, to be effective, requires strong political support, and this is certainly the need in Indonesia today. In one sense, this support is provided by Indonesia's commitment to development, and within this framework, there is considerable political and bureaucratic incentive to solve land problems so they do not hinder development projects and programs.

Unfortunately, this is not an adequate or properly focused level of political support because linking land problems solely with development issues will not bring about the extensive changes needed in the present system of land administration to meet the changing conditions in the country. Thus, if land matters and land problems are to be dealt with effectively, land policy must be given greater political recognition. This would entail raising the visibility of land issues and obtaining the commitment of the government to the changes and the financial support needed to bring about the necessary reforms and improvements in the present system. One way to do this would be to set up a Department for Land Affairs that would have the status of a separate department and access to greater budgetary and staffing allocations. This setup has worked well in other areas. For example, state ministers with their own departments were set up for both environment and research in the 1970s to coordinate and provide adequate bureaucratic backing to policies in these areas. The existence of such ministers raises the visibility and importance of these fields and provides a mechanism for effective policy interaction. Such moves would certainly underline the New Order's commitment to solving the country's growing land problems.

However, it remains questionable whether, given the aims and priorities of the New Order government, any or all of these reforms are possible. Apart from political commitment considerable additional funding would be required at a period when Indonesia faces difficult economic times in the foreseeable future in which funding is being cut back in all areas. Land also remains a sensitive commodity whether it is in the rural areas or in the wealthier urban areas, and in a country that is committed to sustaining internal stability, there is some question as to how far the present government will go in bringing about any radical changes in existing policies.

These reservations should not hold back the process of establishing in the very near future a national land policy. Such a policy can be established in stages, if necessary. The present land administration system needs initial urgent reform to make it more effective, using some of the steps suggested in this book. These can and need to be taken now to overcome the problems that are holding up the very development programs that the present government is fully committed to meeting. The second stage of introducing more extensive changes should then be taken when economic and political conditions improve. Whatever the timing, what is required now is acceptance on the part of the government and policymakers in Indonesia of the overriding need for reforms and for the commitment to the establishment of a fully articulated national land policy allied with the political and bureaucratic commitment to carry it out.

## *Notes*

1. The present regulations provide a detailed schedule of fees and charges to be paid for registration of land. Published schedules specify the amounts to be charged for specific actions (e.g., letter of measurement, replacement certificate), as well as the different fee structures for individuals and legal bodies (e.g., corporations) and for rural and urban lands. Registration fees originally were based on 1 percent of land value. In 1978 the fee for issuing the certificate was changed to a fixed amount, while the cost of the letter of measurement remained based on the cost incurred by Agraria. The only exception to this is for PRONA where special provisions have been made to adjust the fees based on the income level of the applicant and thus his ability to pay.
2. Fees are currently sometimes reduced or even waived for low-income applicants, particularly under PRONA, but this is not based on any generally applicable regulation and tends to be on an ad hoc basis.
3. General property taxes may be supplemented by special measures to strengthen these effects. For example, Taiwan and Chile have vacant land taxes to stimulate development in certain zones, and in Korea, speculative gains in land value are taxed.
4. Collection costs tend to be higher in poorer areas since often several visits must be made to households to ensure collection. Some consideration might therefore be given to exempting all households contributing less than, say, Rp2,500 and redirecting efforts toward ensuring more accurate classification of middle- and upper-income properties.

5. In many parts of the world, betterment, or valorization, taxes are able to recoup most or all the investment costs. Unlike general property taxes, which as noted earlier have often been disappointing, the performance of local betterment levies for specific projects has been impressive (Doebele, Grimes, and Linn 1979). Betterment taxes may be in the form of specific charges whereby the cost of betterment is roughly allocated to households or in the form of an excess-value surcharge whereby increases in the value of land in excess of the increase in unimproved land are taxed (Walters 1983).

6. The current legal basis consists of the Dutch Town Planning Ordinance of 1948 and its accompanying Town Planning Regulations of 1949, supplemented by Regulation of the Minister of Home Affairs No. 4 of 1980. The draft City Planning Law of 1982 (*Undang-Undang Ruang Kota*) should provide, when passed, a far sounder legal basis, but this was still not passed into law at the end of 1985.

# Appendix A

## Procedures for a Cadastral Survey

The Directorate of Land Registration (DPT) presently uses terrestrial and photogrammetric procedures for the measurement of parcels, whether individual or complete villages. Wherever there is existing aerial photography over relatively flat areas, the photogrammetric method is used, and where the terrain is steep and for other areas not having photography, the terrestrial method is used. This appendix describes the procedures of both methods and summarizes their advantages and disadvantages as well as the special procedures for transmigration areas.

### *Terrestrial Method*

1. If the measurement is for an individual parcel, a theodolite (a surveyor's instrument) is set up on a nearby known station, and each of the corners of parcel is measured by stadia (a surveying method for determining distances and differences in elevation) from that station and an angle to another known station or reference point. Should one or more of the corners be blocked from the line of sight, then that (those) corner(s) would be measured by chain from the other observation corners. If only two points can be observed, then one diagonal distance would be measured between opposite corners of the parcel. Should there be no established station, the parcel would be tied to at least two reference points by the same procedures as earlier.

2. If the measurement is for a complete *desa* or more than one *desa*, a traverse net with monumented stations is established around and through the village(s). The traverse net is tied into or may include a known triangulation station(s) or a station of established local coordinates. After establishment of the traverse stations, a theodolite is set

up on the various stations and the measurement of all the parcels is made in the same manner as noted in step 1.

3. After the fieldwork of measuring the parcel(s) is completed, distances along boundary lines and parcel areas are computed from the data recorded in the field books. The parcels are then plotted on base map sheets at a scale of 1:1,000, and sometimes the housing areas are plotted at 1:500 scale. The sheets are then numbered sequentially with identification grids for locating parcels. The parcels show type of title (i.e., *Hak Milik, Hak Pakai*, etc.), title number, boundary measurement, and area in hectares. The parcel drawing is also depicted on the letter of measurement, which is placed in the *Buku Tanah* and in the Register of Letters of Measurement.

## Photogrammetric Method

1. Five to eight relatively flat areas (approximately 10,000 to 12,000 hectares) are selected each year for photogrammetric survey. These areas are covered with precision aerial photography through contracts with Indonesian companies.

2. Before flying, a control base is established by ground survey traverse around and through the area to be photographed. The traverse stations are tied to established triangulation stations with known local coordinate positions. If possible, the known stations are included in the traverse.

3. The traverse stations are monumented and premarked (paneled) with a cross, usually of cloth, that can be observed from the aircraft and that will be distinctive on the aerial photograph. In addition to the traverse stations, supplementary monuments are placed throughout the area and also are premarked.

4. The contractor then flies the area in sequential preplanned flight lines using precise aerial mapping cameras for obtaining the photography at a scale of 1:5,000. The photography is processed by the contractor, and after acceptance, photographic positives, negatives, and paper prints are delivered to the Office of Land Registration (DPT).

5. Personnel of DPT then select sharp photo-identifiable tie points for relatively orienting successive photographs in the line of flight and between flight lines. These points as well as the traverse and supplemental monumented stations are given identifying numbers.

6. Points selected on one photograph are then transferred and marked on all subsequent photographs that contain the same image. This is done by point transfer equipment.

7. These points (known control, supplementary, and tie) are then measured for each photograph on stable film positives using a first order

plotter. Presently, the Wild A8 stereo plotter with automatic printout of the X, Y, and Z coordinates is used for photographic mensuration. The Z coordinate is not measured, but the X and Y coordinates are. The plotted X and Y coordinates are the relative horizontal distance measurements on the photographs for each point measured. The Z, if it is read, is the relative elevation. All three coordinates are at photo scale.

8. Through a semianalytical block adjustment of all the photographs of the project area, the photographic net is adjusted relatively together through the tie points and absolutely to the established traverse control stations. After the block computational parameters are determined, horizontal positions are established for the supplementary monumented stations and the photographic tie points. The results at present are usually in local area coordinate system but are relatively precise.

9. With established positions for all points, the stable base film negative of the photograph can be rectified to an accurate 1:1,000 scale cadastral base. The base should be a stable material such as Mylar or equivalent to allow for accurate lineal and areal measurements of the parcel.

10. As with the terrestrial method, drafted base map sheets are prepared to identify type of title, title number, boundary measurement, and area in hectares for each parcel. Parcel plots are subsequently depicted in the letter of measurement for the *Buku Tanah* and the Register of Letters of Measurement.

## Advantages and Disadvantages of Mapping/Measurement Alternatives

### Terrestrial Method

One of the advantages of the terrestrial method is that precision in measurement of distances is far greater than that in the photogrammetric method because precise equipment used at ground scale can measure to an accuracy of better than 1 part in 1,000. In addition, precise angles from control stations can be measured to *sawah* parcel corners that are in light of sight, and in dry land farming areas, the angle between adjacent lines can be directly and precisely measured. Finally, measurement equipment is used directly in the field, and office space is required only for desks and drafting tables.

One disadvantage is that the procedure is slow. One surveyor, with the assistance of a chain and/or stadia person can cover only 2 to 4 hectares a day. Because of this limitation, targets cannot always be met, particularly when staff are limited in numbers. Another disadvantage is that plentiful equipment is required, and transportation is needed on a regular daily basis from a district Agraria headquarters to the field.

*Photogrammetric Method*

The advantages of this system are that large areas can be mapped accurately for the preparation of controlled photo map bases in a relatively short time, and it is not necessary to go the field for measurements to prepare the base map, except to establish a survey traverse control base for the aerial photographic triangulation. In addition, a relatively small staff can produce map bases for large areas. Also, when a precision photographic negative is reproduced to a controlled base, either by rectification or by orthophotographic process, the parcel imagery is accurately portrayed.

One disadvantage is that although the procedures produce an accurate base map, the accuracy in establishing boundary distances and angles between adjacent boundary lines is not as good as in a field survey. This is due to the much smaller scale of the base on which measurements are made. In addition, much more sophisticated and costly equipment is required than in the terrestrial method as well as more space and maintenance requirements plus more extensive training for the various phases of the photogrammetric process.

## Special Procedures for Transmigration Areas

An area selected for transmigration involves policies and decisions of many offices outside the DPT. The procedures identified here involve only land surveying/mapping.

1. Once a decision has been made to open an area for transmigration, an initial survey/inventory is made by Agraria of the general area under consideration.
2. Based on land-use advice, a survey of the peripheral bounds of the area is performed by the DPT.
3. A detailed layout of the area is prepared by the public works. The land is cleared and the DPT surveys the parcel boundaries according to the detailed site plan.
4. A base map of this layout then becomes the cadastral base for certification and registration on which title, boundary measurement, and parcel area in hectares are identified.

# Appendix B

## Credit Systems in Indonesia and Their Use in Land Certification

There are a number of ways that existing credit programs in Indonesia could be used to help land registration by directly or indirectly linking with them land title requirements. This appendix provides a short summary of these programs with suggestions of how the individual programs might be utilized.

### Lending Agencies

Land title certificates are usually required by banking institutions to prove legal ownership of land. This requirement allows the land to be encumbered by *crediet verband* (security for the credit arrangement). The most important of these banking institutions in providing credit and thus establishing collateral requirements in rural areas is the BRI (Bank Rakyat Indonesia, or Indonesian People's Bank). This state bank operates under the direction of the Bank Indonesia (BI). The BRI's primary mission is to provide financing to village economies with an emphasis on financing cooperatives, rural development projects, farmers, and fishermen. The BRI began to set up banking services in 1969 at the subdistrict level. These units are called *unit desa* banks (BRI Unit Desa). Presently there are about 3,300 BRI Unit Desas operating in Indonesia. In Java and Bali BRI Unit Desas service approximately 600 to 1,000 hectares of well-irrigated rice fields (*sawah*) and about 1,000 to 1,500 hectares in the outer islands. A typical village in Java has about 100 to 200 hectares of well-irrigated rice fields worked by some 200 to 400 rice farmers. Thus, one BRI Unit Desa serves from 6 to 10 villages, roughly equivalent to a subdistrict area.

## Credit Programs

Some of the existing credit programs that could be utilized to generate increased land certification are as follows.

### BIMAS Loan Scheme

In terms of volume of credit and number of accounts, the BIMAS loan program is by far the most important credit program in rural areas. As of the end of 1980, over 4.5 million loan accounts were outstanding, with a total balance outstanding of Rp132 billion (US$215 million). An average loan size is about Rp40,000 (US$65).

The BIMAS program is a credit package coordinated by the Department of Agriculture. The loan is primarily used by the farmer to purchase production inputs such as seed and fertilizer, but there is also an allowance for consumption. One package is generally limited to Rp40,000 (approximately US$65) per hectare, but this figure can vary depending on the area and input requirements.

The collateral policy of the BRI for BIMAS loans depends on the size of the loan. If the loan is for one package (Rp40,000), then no collateral or land title certificate (*sertipikat*) is required. The borrower receives the loan on the basis of the recommendation of the village head and an extension worker (Letter A). Letter A essentially indicates that the borrower is a farmer, has paid land taxes (IPEDA), and is of good character. The security is the income potential and the borrower's character.

If the farmer wants to borrow more than one BIMAS package, land collateral and a certificate are required. The potential borrower may have a certificate to his or her land; if not, he or she will have to apply to Agraria for one. If the certificate cannot be processed in a reasonably short period, Agraria will issue a letter of information (*surat keterangan*) that indicates to the BRI that the certificate is in process and is forthcoming. The borrower can use this letter as proof of ownership.

Thus, with loans of over one BIMAS package the primary security is still the income potential and the borrower's character. Bank policy, however, requires a secondary security, usually land, as the loan amount increases. If a borrower defaults on a loan, the BRI has the authority to take the land and sell it at auction to recover the amount of the loan. Any money left over would be given to the landowner. In practice, though, this is seldom done. The BRI prefers to recover the loan administratively. Apparently this is a policy decision of the government since the primary objective of the credit program is to provide easy credit to cultivate the land, not to acquire it.

The BIMAS program currently does not generate a significant need for certificates because very few of the loans are for over Rp40,000. However, this could be rectified with a certificate required for all loans, whether Rp40,000 or less.

*KIK/KMKP Credit Programs*

Other small credit programs that require collateral from borrowers in rural areas and that could be utilized to create a requirement for certificates are numerous. Two of the important programs in terms of number of accounts and volume of credit are KIK (Kredit Kecil, or Small Investment Credit) and KMKP (Kredit Modal Kerja Permanent, or Small Permanent Working Capital Credit).

The KIK/KMKP program provides medium-term credit for investment (KIK) and permanent working capital (KMKP) to small enterprises across all sectors of the economy. A business is eligible if its net worth, excluding owner-occupied land and buildings, does not exceed Rp100 million in industry and construction of Rp40 million in other sectors. There is a maximum loan limit of Rp10 million each for KIK and for KMKP.

The magnitude of the program and thus the potential demand in rural areas for certificates is illustrated when figures for these programs are examined. In 1980, for instance, 42,417 KIK and 245,758 KMKP loans were approved. Of this total, 1,942 (45.8 percent) of the KIK and 20,742 (84.4 percent) of the KMKP were in the agriculture sector (USAID 1982, p. 73). The KIK loans to agriculture are used to purchase capital equipment and supplies such as tractors, water buffaloes, and water pumps for irrigation. The KMKP loans are used to increase the working capital for crop production, small rice mills, and so forth. Collateral requirements for the KIK/KMKP loans are mainly the assets financed by the loan. Additional collateral up to 50 percent of the loan amount may be secured, if available. Traditionally this additional collateral requirement is land. Thus, when required, the borrower must present a certificate and *crediet verband* must be registered against the certificate/land to obtain the loan. Thus, both these expanding programs present excellent opportunities to link credit with land registration.

*Kredit Mini and Kredit Midi*

Kredit Mini (small credit) and Kredit Midi (medium credit) programs in the rural areas can also generate the need to pledge land for collateral and thus could create a demand for certificates.

Kredit Mini is an extensive loan program. Loans are handled through the village units of the BRI. As of the end of 1980 over a half-million Kredit Mini loans were outstanding with a balance totaling more than Rp30 billion. This is an average balance of about Rp60,000 (US$92) per account. Collateral requirements for the Kredit Mini programs depend on the size of loan and what is purchased, but according to regulations collateral is always required. Since Kredit Mini loans can be as low as Rp10,000 (US$16), the only collateral required might be the tools that are purchased, for example. In large loans (Rp40,000 or more), however, certificates are required as collateral for loans. Collateral requirements for Kredit Midi are the same as for KIK/KMKP credit.

*Credit Schemes for Smallholder Lander Development*

The nucleus estate smallholder program, conversion to rice land program (*pencetakan sawah*), and other smallholder land development programs involve issuance of certificates and the pledging of land as collateral for land development loans.

Of these projects, the nucleus estate and smallholder (NES) program is the largest project funded by the World Bank and other donors in a number of provinces in Java, Sumatra, Sulawesi, and Kalimantan. Certificates are issued to the new settlers as part of the government-sponsored settlement package, and the land can be—and often is—pledged as collateral for land development loans.

## Summary

Land title certificates and *crediet verband* deeds allow land to be pledged as collateral. The need for certificates is currently not significant in the BIMAS program because most loans are for about Rp40,000 and thus do not require certificates. However, this situation could well be adjusted so that all loans would require certification. The KIK/KMKP, the Kredit Mini, and the Kredit Midi generate a need for certificates although only for larger accounts, which given the nature of the program is reasonable. A significant number of certificates are required in rice land conversion (*pencetakan sawah*), nucleus estates smallholders, and other land development schemes. The certificates in these cases are an integral part of the financial arrangements.

In the future if the banks institute a program of mortgage credit (lending money to purchase agriculture land and effecting a mortgage on the purchased land) that currently does not exist, then a significant demand for certificates certainly would ensue.

# Appendix C

## Betterment Taxes in Indonesia

Indonesia in the mid-1980s has only one example of an active betterment tax. This is the Jakarta special tax (*pajak khusus*) that incorporates two of the elements found in betterment taxes worldwide: one in the form of specific charges whereby the cost of betterment is roughly allocated to households and the second in the form of an excess-value surcharge whereby increases in the value of land in excess of the increase in unimproved land are taxed. The tax is currently being extended by the Jakarta city government to provide a potentially significant way of financing new urban infrastructure.

The legislative basis for the *pajak khusus* is a 1972 regulation (Peraturan Daerah No. 1, March 8, 1972) permitting city authorities to recover 60 percent of the cost of new and improved infrastructure (including roads, bridges, drainage, water supply, electricity, etc.) in those areas designated by the governor. The special tax consists of two parts. Part I is in the form of a fixed charge whereby 60 percent of the cost of improvements is divided between the beneficiaries according to the length of road frontage, with properties directly fronting onto the road paying more than those only indirectly connected in the ratio 7:3. Buildings and land used for social and government purposes are excluded. The tax is calculated and announced to taxpayers before the improvements are made and must be paid within 3 years in twelve quarterly installments after the completion of the work. In addition to financial penalties for late payment, no building permit is granted until the tax has been paid.

Part II of the *pajak khusus* is an explicit tax on excessive increases in land prices due to betterment. If the value of a parcel of land increases by more than 300 percent within 2 years of the completion of the work, a charge of 50 percent is imposed on all increases above the 300 percent price increase. This tax is collected on change of ownership.

Part I of the *pajak khusus* has been fairly successful in recovering costs in the small number of areas of Jakarta where it has been approved. For example, in Tebet, the first area where the tax was collected, 47 percent of the cost of betterment was collected between 1974 and 1980, which is equivalent to 79 percent of the potential collection. The average assessment was Rp110,000 per plot, and most (about 83 percent) was collected in the first 3 years. These figures are fairly representative of subsequent efforts; for more recent periods the average assessments have risen to Rp200,000 to Rp300,000, and in some cases collection rates of 90 to 95 percent have been achieved. However, the total amount collected remains small. In the 7 year period of 1974/1975 to 1980/1981, only Rp750 million was collected. Since then receipts have risen, reaching Rp192 million in 1982/1983 and are budgeted for Rp330 million in 1983/1984. Part II of the *pajak khusus* until now has never been implemented (World Bank 1985, p. 189).

The *pajak khusus* tax is well designed in principle, but a number of practical problems involved tend to reduce its effectiveness. These include late notification of the tax department that an area will be improved and consequent late notification of landholders, difficulties in tracing landholders because of unregistered land transactions, and a lack of data on land values and of staff to collect these data. A number of procedures could significantly raise collections: For example, publicity in areas scheduled for betterment could be increased, and sign boards should make clear what the tax is, who is responsible for paying, and that no land may be transferred without payment.

The tax is currently designated to recover only 60 percent of the cost of improvements. Given that some taxes are not collected and that 3 years are allowed for tax payments (without adding interest charges), the *pajak khusus* collects at most 50 percent of any improvement costs. The *pajak khusus* clearly could be raised without putting an unfair burden on the poorer beneficiaries. While further study should be undertaken on this question, the evidence from Jakarta suggests that as long as standards are not set too high, construction takes place in stages, and the major burden is placed on middle- and upper-income beneficiaries, betterment levies are easily affordable (World Bank 1984, p. 189). The excess-value surcharge (Part II of the *pajak khusus*) also provides good potential for raising cost recovery with the great attraction that it is not a burden on anybody, however poor. Since it is only levied at the time of land sale, it effectively pays for itself since funds from the sale are used to pay the tax. Evidence showed that when government improvement programs are provided to poorly served *kampungs*, there is roughly a doubling of land prices, while the construction of an access road may cause prices of adjacent land to triple (ibid., p. 198).

On both economic and social grounds, it is highly desirable that betterment taxes be extended in Indonesia so they can be used to pay for the increasing urban development costs. From an equity standpoint, betterment charges permit a redistribution of income and can prevent some of the regressive income distribution effects of betterment. The effects on land prices of public investments can be substantial; currently upper-income landowners not only enjoy the improved facilities but also can make substantial gains when selling the land. Large landowners therefore benefit much more than small land-owners; this is particularly true in Indonesian cities where rich and poor homes tend to be mixed together much more than in most countries. Because of this situation, it is very difficult to direct upgrading programs specifically toward the poor. Betterment taxes can prevent these disproportionate gains from accruing to the better off. In addition, to the extent that charges are levied for betterment, land prices will stay lower, resulting in consequent social and economic advantages.

# Glossary

**Adat**  Customary or traditional law.

**Agraria**  See Agrarian Affairs.

**Agrarian Affairs**  Refers to the Department of Agrarian Affairs in the 1960s and then to the part of the Department of Home Affairs that took over the administration of land affairs in the 1970s, i.e. the Directorate General of Agrarian Affairs (Agraria) and the Agrarian Affairs (Agraria) offices in the provinces and districts.

**Alang-alang (Imperata cylindrica)**  A flat-bladed coarse weed growing in an area abandoned by shifting cultivators.

**BAPPENAS**  Badan Perencanaan Nasional, National Planning Board.

**Bengkok**  Land provided to village officials in lieu of salary.

**BI**  Bank Indonesia, the central bank.

**Bimas**  Bimbingan Massal, agricultural intensification program (primarily rice production).

**BKK**  Badan Kredit Kecamatan, subdistrict (*kecamatan*) credit body.

**BRI**  Bank Rakyat Indonesia, government-owned bank primarily responsible for distributing agriculture credit in rural areas.

**BUD**  Bank Unit Desa, branch of the BRI at the subdistrict (*kecamatan*) level.

**BULOG**  Badan Urusan Logistik, Logistics Board responsible for procuring and distributing various basic commodities, of which the most important is rice.

**Bupati**  Chief administrative official of a *kabupaten* (district).

**BUUD**  Badan Usaha Unit Desa, government-supported village organization established to assist in distributing farm inputs and purchasing rice and other crops.

**Cadastre**  Land Survey usually carried out as part of land registration and titling process.

**Camat**  Chief administrative official of *kecamatan* (subdistrict).

**Crediet Verband**   Security for credit arrangement.

**Department**   Term used for a central government ministry in Indonesia.

**Desa**   Village.

**DKI**   Daerah Khusus Ibukota, special area of Jakarta, which has the administrative status of province.

**DPA**   Dewan Pertimbangan Agung or Supreme Advisory Council.

**DPR**   Dewan Perwakilan Rakyat or People's Representative Assembly.

**DPT**   Direktorat Pendaftaran Tanah, Directorate of Land Registration.

**Gadai**   Transfer of land for cash with retention of option to recover the land by repayment (pawning).

**GBHN**   Garis Besar Haluan Negara, state guidelines for national policy.

**GLD**   Guided Land Development Scheme used to develop peripherary urban areas by providing basic infrastructure to private land owners on outskirts of urban areas to encourage sale, lease or subdivision of land for residential use.

**Gotong Royong**   Mutual self-help programs.

**Hak Gadai**   Land pledge.

**Hak Guna Usaha**   The right of exploitation under Article 16 of Basic Agrarian Law (BAL) No. 5 of 1960.

**Hak Membuka Tanah**   Short-term, temporary period under the BAL to open up land.

**Hak Milik Adat**   Customary full ownership right.

**Hak Pakai**   The right of use under Article 16 of BAL No. 5 of 1960.

**Hak pengelolaan**   The right of management.

**Hipotik**   A mortgage (from Dutch *hypotheque*).

**Hukum Adat**   Traditional law of the community.

**IBRD**   International Bank for Reconstruction and Development (The World Bank).

**Ijon System**   System of selling crops before harvest time to receive prepayment.

**Inmas**   Intensifikasi massal, agricultural extension program for rice and other food crops; the Inmas program, in contrast to Bimas, does not provide credit to participants but supplies them with subsidized inputs.

**Inpres**   Instruksi President, program carried out on the basis of presidential instruction, usually for infrastructure works containing a substantial job-creation element.

**IPEDA**   Iuran Pembangunan Daerah, the main land tax.

**Jual-beli Tanah**   Free purchase or sale of land.

**Kabupaten**   Subprovincial (district) administrative unit.

**Kabupaten Program**   District-level support program started in 1961.

**Kampung**   Subdivision of a village.

**Kecamatan**   Subdistrict administrative unit below a *kabupaten*.

**Kelurahan**   Administrative unit below the *kecamatan*, often the same as a *desa*.

**Kepala Desa**   Head of the village.

**KIK**   Kredit Investasi Kecil, Small Investors' Credit.

**KMKP**   Kredit Modal Kerja Permanen, Permanent Working Capital Credit.

***Kotamadya*** Municipality; having the same administrative status as a *kabupaten*.

***Kredit Midi*** Small to medium credit scheme with limit of Rp500,000 of Bank Rakyat Indonesia.

***Kredit Mini*** Small credit scheme with limit of Rp200,000 of Bank Rakyat Indonesia.

***Ladang*** Land used for dry field farming by shifting cultivation.

***Lurah*** Elected village head in Java.

***Marga*** A community group.

**MPR** Majelis Permusyawaratan Rakyat, National Assembly.

**Negative Land Registration System** System where land registration provides only strong evidence of ownership.

**NES** Nucleus Estate and Smallholder project, smallholder land development projects (primarily rubber).

**New Order Period** Period from 1965/1966 until present during which President Soeharto has held office.

***Notaris*** Land deed official.

**Office on Wheels** Concept of a mobile land registration (land) office.

**Old Order Period** Pre–New Order period, refers to the era in which President Soekarno was in office.

**Padat Karya** Rural Works Program started in 1972.

***Padi*** Unthreshed rice that is harvested and can be tied into bundles with part of the stalk.

***Palawija*** Nonrice food crops, chief among which are corn, and cassava.

***Pancasila*** The five principles of the Republic of Indonesia: belief in God, national consciousness, humanitarianism, social justice, democracy.

***Pencetakan Sawah*** Land that is converted to wet rice fields through special government program.

***Perkebunan*** Commercial tree, bush, or field crop plantation (estate).

***Petani*** Farmer.

***Petuk Pajak*** Land tax certificate.

***Repelita*** Rencana Pembangunan Lima Tahun, five-year development plan.

**Repelita I** First Five-Year Development Plan, 1969/1970–1973/1974.

**Repelita II** Second Five-Year Development Plan, 1974/1975–1978/1979.

**Repelita III** Third Five-Year Development Plan, 1979/1980–1983/1984.

**Repelita IV** Fourth Five-Year Development Plan, 1984/1985–1988/1989.

**Repelita V** Fifth Five-Year Development Plan, 1989/1990–1993/1994.

***Sawah*** Irrigated rice field.

***Sertipikat*** Certificated title issued under the BAL of 1960.

**Subsidy Desa** Village-Subsidy program started in 1970s.

***Surat Keterangan*** Letter of information regarding land rights.

***Surat ukur*** Letter of land measurement.

***tanah Bengkok*** Land given to village official to be used for salary.

***tanah Darat*** Term used by IPEDA to designate land other than *sawah*.

***tanah Desa*** Village land, the income of which goes to the village treasury.

*tanah kering*   Dry land for cultivation.
*tanah Mesjid*   Mosque land.
*tanah Milik*   Privately owned land.
*tanah negara*   State-owned land.
*tanah Pekuburan*   Cemetery land.
*tanah Pusaka*   Ancestral land.
*tanah Swapraja*   Land belonging to former native rulers.
*tegalan*   Dry land cultivated on a more or less permanent basis.
*Ulayat*   Right of disposition over land enjoyed by local community.

# Bibliography

## Books and Articles

Abey, A.; A. Booth and R. M. Sundrum. 1981. "Labour Absorption in Indonesia Agriculture." *Bulletin of Indonesian Economic Studies* 17(1):36–60.

Agro Economic Survey. 1977. "Rural Labor Market Survey." Mimeographed. Bogor: Agro Economic Survey.

Agro Economic Survey. 1984. "Rural Labor Market Survey." Mimeographed. Bogor: Agro Economic Survey.

Agro Ekonomi, n.d. "Pola Pengusahaan Tanah, Hubungan Kerja Pertanian dan Distribusi Pendapatan di Pedesaan Jawa [Land Use Patterns, The Relationships Between Agricultural Activities and Income Distribution in Javanese Villages]." Mimeographed. Bogor: Agro Economic Survey.

Alderman, H., and C. P. Timmer. 1980. "Food Policy and Food Demand in Indonesia." *Bulletin of Indonesian Economic Studies* 16(3):83–93.

Andi Lolo, T. R. 1979. "Masyarakat Jawa Area Transmigrasi [The Javanese Society in the Transmigration Areas]." Mimeographed. Social Science Research Training Center: Ujung Pandang.

Babcock, T. 1986. "Transmigration as a Regional Development Strategy." In C. MacAndrews, ed., *Central Government and Local Development in Indonesia*. Kuala Lumpur: Oxford University Press, 126–144.

Bagyo, A. S., and J. Lingard. 1983. "The Impact of Agricultural Mechanization on Production and Employment in Rice Areas of West Java." *Bulletin of Indonesian Economic Studies* 19(1):53–67.

Barlow, C., and Murhaminto. 1982. "The Rubber Smallholder Economy." *Bulletin of Indonesian Economic Studies* 18(2):86–119.

Basuki, S. 1976. "Penyediaan Tanah untuk Keperluan Perusahaan dan Beberapa Masalah Pertanahan di Pedesaan [Land Provision for Industrial Purposes and Land Problems in the Villages]." Mimeographed. Centre of Trade Law Studies, Faculty of Law University of Indonesia.

Birowo, A., and G.H. Hansen. 1981. "Agricultural and Rural Development, An Overview" in Gary E. Hansen, ed., *Agricultural and Rural Development in Indonesia*. Boulder, Colorado: Westview Press, pp. 1–30.

Boerhan, B. and S. Thalib. 1977. "Pengaruh Undang-Undang Pokok Agraria Terhadap Tanah Adat di Sumatera Barat [The Impact of Basic Agrarian Law on Tribal Land in West Sumatra]. Mimeographed. West Sumatra: Faculty of Law, University of Andalas.

Booth, A. 1974. "Land Ownership in Klaten." *Bulletin of Indonesian Economic Studies* 10(3):135–140.

Booth, A. 1979. "The Agricultural Surveys, 1970–75." *Bulletin of Indonesian Economic Studies* 15(1):24–39.

Booth, A. 1981. "The Role of Agricultural Taxation." in Gary E. Hansen, *Agricultural and Rural Development in Indonesia*. Boulder, Colorado: Westview Press, pp. 44–64.

Booth, A., and P. McCawley. 1981. *The Indonesian Economy During the Soeharto Era*. Kuala Lumpur: Oxford University Press.

Booth, A., and R.M. Sundrum. 1976. "The 1973 Agricultural Census." *Bulletin of Indonesian Economic Studies* 22(2): 90–105.

Booth, A., and R.M. Sundrum. 1981. "Income Distribution." in Booth and McCawley, eds., *The Indonesian Economy under the Soeharto Era*. Kuala Lumpur: Oxford University Press, pp. 181–217.

Bowen, J. 1982. "Land Tenure and Village Structure, in Aceh." Mimeographed. Banda Aceh: Development Alternatives Inc.

Burbridge, P.; J. Dixon; and B. Soewardi. 1981. "Land Allocation for Transmigration." *Bulletin of Indonesian Economic Studies* 17(1):108–113.

Bureau of Statistics. Government of Indonesia 1963. *Agricultural Census*, Vol. 1. Jakarta.

Bureau of Statistics. Government of Indonesia 1972. *Population Census 1971: Series B, No. 2*. Jakarta.

Bureau of Statistics. Government of Indonesia 1973. *Agricultural Census*. Jakarta.

Bureau of Statistics. Government of Indonesia 1975. *Statistical Year Book of Indonesia*. Jakarta.

Bureau of Statistics. Government of Indonesia 1982. *Statistical Year Book of Indonesia*. Jakarta.

Bureau of Statistics. Government of Indonesia 1984. *Statistical Year Book of Indonesia*. Jakarta.

Clohessy, E. 1983. "Legal View of Opportunities for Acceleration of Land Registration in the Rural Areas of Indonesia." Jakarta: U.S. Agency for International Development (USAID).

Collier, W.L. 1980. "Social and Economic Aspects of Tidal Swamp Land Development in Indonesia," Occasional Paper No. 151. Development Studies Center: The Australian National University.

Collier, W.L.; H. Hadikoesworo; and S. Saropie. 1977. "Income, Employment and Food Systems in Javanese Coastal Villages." South East Asian Series No. 44. Athens, Ohio: Ohio University, Center for International Studies.

Collier, W. L.; Sri Hartoyo; and Soentoro. 1981. "Land Tenure and Labor Markets in East Java Indonesia." Mimeographed. Bogor: Agro Economic Survey.

Day, C. 1966. *The Dutch in Java*. London: Oxford University Press.

Department of Finance. 1982. *Nota Keungan* [Financial Notes]. Jakarta.

Department of Information. 1985. *Repelita IV—The Fourth Five Year Development Plan 1984/85–1988/89*. Jakarta.

Department of Information. 1984. "Indonesia." Jakarta.

Department of Labour, Transmigration and Cooperatives. 1977. "Proyek Penelitian Bentuk-Bentuk Interaksi Sosial Antar Kelompok Etnis di Daerah Transmigrasi [Research Project on Socio-Economic Interactions Among the Ethnic Groups in Transmigration Areas]." Mimeographed. Jakarta.

De Witt, J. B. 1973. "The Kabupaten Program." *Bulletin of Indonesian Economic Studies* 9(1):65–85.

Directorate General of Agrarian Affairs, Department of Home Affairs. n.d. "Uraian Umum Mengenai Pendaftaran Tanah [General Analysis of Land Registration]." Mimeographed. Jakarta.

Directorate General of Irrigation, Department of Public Works. 1977. "Masalah-Masalah Tanah dalam Hubungannya dengan Proyek-Proyek Pengairan [Land Problems in The Irrigation Projects]." Mimeographed. Jakarta.

Directorate General of Transmigration. 1972. "Pattern of Policies in the Implementation of Transmigration." Mimeographed. Jakarta.

Directorate General of Transmigration. 1975. "Laporan Survey Indetifikasi Daerah Transmigrasi Pematang Panggang Kabupaten Komering Ilir [Report on a Transmigration Area Identification Survey in Pematang Panggang of Komering Ilir District]." Mimeographed. Jakarta.

Doebele, W. A.; O. F. Grimes; and J. F. Linn. 1979. "Participation of Beneficiaries in Financing Urban Services," *Land Economics*, no. 55. Madison: University of Wisconsin, pp. 3–92.

Dove, M. 1980. "Myth and Method in the Study of Shifting Cultivation." Mimeographed. Yogyakarta: University of Gadjah Mada.

Dove, M. 1982. "The Myth of the Communal Long House in Rural Development, the Kantu of West Kalimantan." In Colin MacAndrews and L.S. Chia, eds., *Too Rapid Rural Development*. Athens: Ohio University Press, pp. 14–78.

Dove, M. 1986. "The Ideology of Agricultural Development in Indonesia; in Colin MacAndrews, ed., *Central Government and Local Development in Indonesia*. Kuala Lumpur: Oxford University Press, pp. 121–140.

Dris, D. 1969. "Taxation in Indonesia." *Ekonomi dan Keuangan* [Economy and Finance] Indonesia, (59):19–31.

Elson, R.E. 1978. "The Cultivation System and 'Agricultural Involution'." Working Paper No. 14. Australia: Monash University Centre of Southeast Asian Studies.

Faculty of Law, University of Hasanuddin. 1977. "Pengaruh Undang-Undang Pokok Agraria Terhadap Tanah Adat di Daerah Sulawesi Selatan [The

Impact of Basic Agrarian Law on Tribal Land in South Sulawesi]." Mimeographed. Ujung Pandang.

Faculty of Law, University of Lambung Mangkurat. 1977. "Pengaruh Undang-Undang Pokok Agraria Terhadap Tanah Adat di Daerah Kalimantan Selatan [The Impact of Basic Agrarian Law on Tribal Land in South Kalimantan]." Banjarmasin.

Faculty of Law, University of North Sumatra. 1977. "Pengaruh Undang-Undang Pokok Agraria Terhadap Tanah Adat di Sumatera Utara [The Impact of Basic Agrarian Law on Tribal Land in North Sumatra]." Medan.

Faculty of Law, University of Syah Kuala, Aceh, Indonesia. n.d. "Pengaruh Undang-Undang Pokok Agraria Terhadap Tanah Adat di Daerah Istimewa Aceh [The Impact of Basic Agrarian Law on Tribal Land in Aceh]." Mimeographed.

Fisher, B.H. and A. M. Ibrahim. 1979. "Regional Development Studies and Planning in Indonesia." *Bulletin of Indonesian Economic Studies*, 15(2):113–127.

Fox, J. 1976. "Report on Second Visit to NTT and Project Area for NTT Pilot Livestock Development Project." Mimeographed. Jakarta.

Fox, J. 1977. *Harvest of the Palm: Ecological Change in Eastern Indonesia.* Cambridge, Mass.: Harvard University Press.

Furnivall, J.S. 1944. *Netherlands India: A Study of Plural Economy.* Cambridge, Mass.: Cambridge University Press.

Gautama, S. n.d. "Masalah Agraria Berikut Peraturan-Peraturan dan Contoh-Contoh [Agrarian Problems Including the Regulations and Examples]." Mimeographed. Bandung.

Gautama, S. and B. Harsono. 1972. "Agrarian Law." Bandung: Faculty of Law, University of Padjadjaran.

Gautama, S. and R.N. Hornick. 1974. *An Introduction to Indonesian Law.* Bandung: Penerbit Alumni.

GBHN–Garis Besar Haluan Negara [Guidelines of State Policy]. 1983. Jakarta: Department of Information.

German Technical Cooperation. 1976. "West Sumatra Regional Development, Agriculture Development Project." Project Report. Bukit Tinggi.

Gertz, C. 1963. *Agricultural Involution.* Berkeley: University of California Press.

Hansen, G.E., ed., 1981. *Agricultural and Rural Development in Indonesia.* Boulder, Colorado: Westview Press.

Hayami, Y. and A. Hafid. 1979. "Rice Harvesting and Welfare in Rural Java." *Bulletin of Indonesian Economic Studies* 15(2):94–112.

Holland, D. 1971. "Report on the Revenue Structure of the City of Jakarta." Mimeographed. Jakarta Real Estate Tax Project. Jakarta, Indonesia.

Hudson, A.B. 1974. "Swidden Systems and Agricultural Development, A Case Study from Kalimantan." Paper presented at the Conference of Indonesian Agricultural Development in July, Madison, Wisconsin.

Huizer, G. 1974. "Peasant Mobilization and Land Reform in Indonesia." Occasional Paper. The Hague: Institute of Social Studies.

Indonesia. 1960. "Peraturan Dasar Pokok-Pokok Agraria dan Landreform [Basic Principles of Land and Landreform]." Special Issue no. 169, January. Jakarta: Department of Information.
Jabotabek Metropolitan Development Plan. 1980. Directorate General of Human Settlements, Department of Public Works, Jakarta.
Jay, R. 1969. *Javanese Villages*. Cambridge, Mass.: MIT Press.
Jeffries, A. 1980. "The Design and Implementation of a System of Market-Based Urban Property Valuation in Surabaya." Jakarta: Indonesia Department of Finance.
Jones, G.W. 1981. "Labour Force Development since 1961." In Anne Booth and Peter McCawley, eds., *The Indonesian Economy During Soeharto Era*. Kuala Lumpur: Oxford University Press, pp. 218–254.
Kasryno, F. 1981. "Land Tenure and Labor Relations in West Java, Indonesia. A Case Study in Four Villages." Mimeographed. Bogor: Agro Economic Survey.
Kaye, L. 1985. "Indonesia Drifts As The Oil Tide Ebbs," in *Far Eastern Economic Review*, Hongkong, November 14, p. 67.
Koentjaraningrat ed.. 1967. *Villages in Indonesia*. Cornell University Press, Ithaca.
Krinks, P.A. 1978. "Rural Changes in Java: An End to Involution." *Geography* 63(1):31–36, London.
Kumar, A. 1980. "The Peasantry and the State on Java: Changes in Relationships, Seventeenth to Nineteenth Centuries." in J.A.C. MacKie, ed., *Indonesia; Australian Perspectives* Vol. III. Canberra: Australian National University, pp. 577–600.
Kuntowijoyo. 1980. "Social Change in Agrarian Society. Madura 1850–1940." Ph.D. dissertation, Columbia University, New York.
Ladjinski, W. 1977. "Land Reform in Indonesia." In L.J. Walinksy, ed., *Agrarian Reform as Unfinished Business*, London: Oxford University Press.
Lerche, D. 1972. "Membiayai Pembangunan Perkotaan Kasus Pengetrapan Pajak Tanah dan Bangunan Secara Efektip [Financing The City Development, Case Study on Land and Building Taxes Effective Application]," *Prisma* (7):11–18, Jakarta.
Lerche, D. 1974. "Notes on Land and Property Taxation in Indonesia." In *Land Taxation in Indonesia:* Report of the Jakarta Real Estate Tax Project. Jakarta.
Lerche, D. 1976. "The Revenue Potential of the Land Tax for Urban Finance in Indonesia." In John Wong, ed., *The Cities of Asia; A Study of Urban Solutions and Urban Finance*. Singapore: Singapore University Press, pp. 315–350.
Lyon, M. 1970. "The Basis of Conflict in Rural Java." Monograph No. 3. Berkeley: Center for South and Southeast Asia Studies, University of California.
MacAndrews, C. 1978. "Transmigration in Indonesia." *Asian Survey* 18(5):458–472.
MacAndrews, C., ed., 1986. "Central Government and Local Development in Indonesia." Kuala Lumpur: Oxford University Press.

MacAndrews, C. and L.S. Chia, ed., 1982. "Too Rapid Rural Development." Athens, Ohio: Ohio University Press.

MacAndrews, C. and S. Soeroto. 1979. "Land Affairs in Indonesia: An Annotated Bibliography." Yogyakarta: Institute for Rural and Regional Studies, University of Gadjah Mada.

Madjalah H.P. [Journal of Law]. 1978. "Hukum dan Keadilan [Law and Justice]." *Jakarta Year IV* (4):17–21.

Menteri Agraria (Minister of Land Affairs). 1964. "Laporan Tentang Masalah Tanah [Report on Land Problems]." Jakarta.

Menteri Agraria (Minister of Land Affairs). 1965. *Laporan: Pelaksanaan Landreform dan Problem-Problemnya* [Land Reform Implementation and Its Problems]. Jakarta.

Metzner, J.K. 1976. "Lamtoronisasi: An Experiment in Soil Conservation." *Bulletin of Indonesian Economic Studies* 7(1):103–109.

Ministry of Research. 1978. "Masalah Pertanahan Laporan Kepada President [Land Problems, Report to President]." Jakarta.

Ministry of Research. 1978. "Masalah Pertanahan dengan Surat-Surat Keputusan Bersama antara Menteri Ekuin dan Bappenas [Land Problems and Decision Letters by the Minister of Economics and Finance and the Minister of National Development Planning]." Jakarta.

Montgomery, R. 1975. "Migration, Employment and Unemployment in Java: Changes from 1961 to 1971 with Particular Reference to the Green Revolution." *Asian Survey* 15(3):222–233.

Montgomery, R. and T. Sugito. 1975. "Changes in the Structure of Farms and Farming in Indonesia between Censuses (1963–1973) and Initial insights on the Issue of Inequality and Near Landlessness." Mimeo - graphed. Jakarta: Ford Foundation.

Morfit, M. 1986. "Pancasila Orthodoxy." In Colin MacAndrews, ed., *Central Government and Local Development in Indonesia*. Kuala Lumpur: Oxford University Press, pp. 46–61.

Morris, R. 1975. "The Potential Impact of Mechanical Land Preparation in the Indonesian Small-holder Production Sector." Los Banos: International Rice Research Institute.

Mortimer, R. 1972. "The Indonesian Communist Party and Land Reform 1959–1965." Monash University Papers on Southeast Asia No. 1. Clayton, Australia.

Mortimer, R., ed., 1973. *Indonesia; 'Showcase State.'* Sydney, Australia: Angus & Robertson.

Mortimer, R., ed., 1976. "The Place of Communism." In E. McVay, ed., *Studies in Indonesian History*. Victoria, Australia: Pitmans.

Mubyarto. 1977. "The Sugar Industry: From Estate to Smallholder Cane Production." *Bulletin of Indonesian Economic Studies* 8(2):29–44.

NUDS (National Urban Development Strategy) Project. 1985. Final Report, September. Jakarta: Directorate General of Human Settlement, Department Public Works.

Oldman, D. and R. Holland. 1972. "Jakarta Real Estate Tax Study; Final Report." Jakarta: Department of Finance, Government of Indonesia.

Pacubas, S.A. 1983. "The Legal Aspect of Land Mapping, Titling and Registration in Indonesia." Jakarta: United States Agency for International Development (USAID).

Penny, D.H. 1966. "The Economics of Peasant Agriculture: The Indonesian Case." *Bulletin of Indonesian Economic Studies* (5):22–42.

Penny, D.H. and M. Singarimbun. 1973. "Population and Poverty in Rural Java: Some Economic Arithmetic from Sriharjo." Ithaca, N.Y.: Cornell International Agricultural Development Monograph 41, Department of Agricultural Economics, Cornell University.

Raffles, T.S. 1817. *The History of Java.*London: William Murray & Co. Kuala Lumpur: Oxford University Press, reprinted, 1965.

Rashid, N.A. 1978. "Land Law and Land Administration." Mimeographed. Kuala Lumpur: University of Malaya.

Ratnatunga, R.T. 1975. "Land Tenure Activities for Pematang Panggang Project." Jakarta: Direktorat Jenderal Transmigrasi [Directorate General of Transmigration].

Ratnatunga, R.T. 1976. "Land Tenure Activities for the Pematang Panggang Project." UNDP/FAO Project Working Document. Jakarta.

Ratnatunga, R.T. 1975. "Land Tenure in the Province of South East Sulawesi." Jakarta: Direktorat Jenderal Transmigrasi [Directorate General of Transmigration].

Ratnatunga, R.T. 1976. "Preliminary Study of Land Tenure in West Sumatra." UNDP/FAO Project Working Document. Jakarta.

Ratnatunga, R.T. and N. Suastha. 1976. "A Preliminary Study of Land Tenure in the Province of Bengkulu." Jakarta: Direktorat Jenderal Transmigrasi [Directorate General of Transmigration].

Rifai, T.B. n.d. "Bentuk Milik Tanah dan Tingkat Kemakmuran Penyelidikan Pedesaan di Daerah Pati, Jateng [The System of Land Ownership and Survey on Village Living Standard in Pati, Central Java]." Jakarta: Universitas Indonesia.

Rosenberg, J., and D.A. Rosenberg. 1980. *Landless Peasants and Rural Poverty in Indonesia and The Philippines.* Ithaca, N.Y.: Cornell University Press.

Ross, M.S. 1984. "Forestry and Land Use in Indonesia." PhD. Thesis. Oxford University, Oxford, England.

Ruzieka, I. 1979. "Rent Appropriation in Indonesia Logging: East Kalimantan 1972/3–1976/7." *Bulletin of Indonesian Economic Studies* 15(2):45–74.

Sadler, L.E. 1983. "Mapping and Surveying for Land Mapping, Titling and Registration Projects." Jakarta: U.S. Agency for International Development (USAID).

Sajogyo. 1977. "Golongan Miskin dan Partisipasinya dalam Pembangunan Desa [The Poor and Their Participation in Village Development]." *Prisma* (9):24–34.

Sajogyo. 1977. "Human Settlement and Land Use in Rural Areas." Paper presented at the Workshop on National Policies in Human Settlement, Cisarua, West Java, July 25–27, 1977.

Sandy, I.M. 1983. "The Indonesian Land Base and How It Has Changed Agriculture." Paper presented at 34th Annual Congress, International Real Estate Federation, Jakarta, October 1983.

Scholz, U. 1971. "Some Considerations about Land Use in the Province of West Sumatra." Mimeographed. Padang: Provincial Government of West Sumatra.

Scott, J.C. 1976. *The Moral Economy of the Peasant: Rebellion and Subsistence in Southeast Asia.* New Haven: Yale University Press.

Shoup, D. 1983. "Taxation and Public Ownership of Land," In Harold B. Dunkerly, ed., *Urban Land Policy–Issues and Opportunities.* New York: Oxford University Press, pp. 114–129.

Sie, K.S. 1968. "Prospects for Agricultural Development in Indonesia: With Special Reference to Java." Wageningen: Center for Agricultural Publishing and Documentation of Wageningen.

Smith, T. 1970. "The Political Economy of Regional and Urban Revenue Policy in Indonesia." Mimeographed. Jakarta: Ford Foundation.

Smith, T. 1971."Municipal Finance." *Bulletin of Indonesian Economic Studies* 7(1):114–130.

Soedargo. 1973. "Hukum Agraria dalam Era Pembangunan [Agrarian Law in the Development Era]." *Prisma* (6):12–21.

Soekarno. 1959. "Manifesto Politik Republik Indonesia [Political Manifesto of the Republic of Indonesia]," August 17th, Department of Information, Special Issue No. 76.

Soeprapto. 1977. "Undang-Undang Pokok Agraria dalam Praktek Serta Permasalahannya [Basic Agrarian Law in Practice and Its Problems]." Direktorat Jenderal Agraria [Directorate General for Agrarian Affairs]. Jakarta: Department of Home Affairs.

Soeprapto. 1978. "Uraian Singkat Tentang Pelaksanaan Landreform di Indonesia [Brief Analysis on The Landreform Implementation in Indonesia]." Direktorat Jenderal Agraria [Directorate General for Agrarian Affairs]. Jakarta: Department of Home Affairs.

Strout, A.M. 1983. "How Productive are the Soils of Java?" *Bulletin of Indonesian Economic Studies* 19(1):32–50.

Sweeting, P. 1980. "Adat Law and Customs in Bengkulu." Mimeographed. Jakarta.

Ter Haar, B. 1948. "Adat Law in Indonesia." E.A. Hoebel and A.A. Schuller, trans. New York: Institute of Pacific Relations.

Tjondronegoro, S.M.P. 1972. "Land Reform or Land Settlement: Shifts in Indonesian Land Policy 1960–1970." Land Tenure Center, Occasional Paper No. 81. Madison: University of Wisconsin.

Tjondronegoro, S. M.P. 1976. "Beberapa Segi Potensi Sosial Daerah Pedesaan [Village Socio Economic Potentials]." *Journal of Social Research* (1):19–30. Jakarta.

Tjondronegoro, S. M.P. 1984. *Social Organization and Planned Development in Rural Java.* Kuala Lumpur: Oxford University Press.

University of Wisconsin. 1981. "Land Tenure and Agrarian Reform in East and Southeast Asia: An Annotated Bibliography." Land Tenure Center. Madison: University of Wisconsin.

USAID (United States Agency for International Development) and Directorate General of Home Affairs. 1982. "Land Mapping, Titling and Registration in Indonesia." Mimeographed. Jakarta.

Utrecht, E. 1969. "Land Reform in Indonesia." *Bulletin of Indonesian Economic Studies* (3):71–88.

Utrecht, E. 1976. "Political Mobilization of Peasants in Indonesia." *Journal of Contemporary Asia* 6(3A):41–58.

Van Niel, J. 1972. "Measurement of Change under the Cultivation System." *Indonesia* 14:89–109, October 1972. Ithaca, N.Y.: Cornell University.

Waite, D. 1980. "Land Registration: Socio Economic Benefits and Priorities in Rural Indonesia." Mimeographed. Jakarta: United States Agency for International Development (USAID).

Walters, A. 1983. "The Value of Land," In Harold B. Dunkerley, ed., *"Urban Land Policy—Issues and Opportunities."* New York: Oxford University Press. pp. 94—110.

Wertheim, W.F. 1964. *Indonesian Society in Transition: A Study of Social Change.* The Hague: W. van Hoeve.

Wertheim, W.F. and G. Siauw. 1962. "Social Change in Java, 1900–1930," *Pacific Affairs* (35):110–126.

White, B. 1978. "Political Aspects of Poverty, Income Distribution and Their Measurement: Some Examples from Rural Java," Series No. 5. Bogor: Agro-Economic Survey.

Widya Utami and J. Ihalauw. 1973. "Some Consequences of Small Farm Size," *Bulletin of Indonesian Economic Studies* 9(2):64–76.

Wijaya, H. and N.H. Sturgess. 1979. "Land Leasing in East Java." *Bulletin of Indonesian Economic Studies* 15(2):75–89.

World Bank. 1974. *Agricultural Sector Survey, Indonesia.* Washington, D.C.

World Bank. 1975. *Land Reform.* Sector Policy Paper. Washington, D.C.

World Bank. 1984. *Indonesia: Urban Services Sector Report.* Washington, D.C.

World Bank. 1985. *Indonesia: Policies for Growth and Employment.* Washington, D.C.

## Government of Indonesia Laws and Decrees

Law No. 2, (BAL) January 7, 1960, concerning sharecropping agreement.

Law No. 5, (BAL) September 24, 1960, concerning the fundamentals of Agrarian Law.

Regulation No. 2 of Minister of Agrarian Affairs, October 19, 1960, concerning the execution of certain provisions in the Basic Agrarian Law (BAL).

Government Regulation No. 51, December 14, 1960, concerning prohibition of land occupation without consent of the owner or his or her proxy.

Decision of the Minister of Agrarian Affairs, December 31, 1960, concerning the fixation of maximum areas on agricultural land.

Regulation No. 56, December 29, 1960, imposing a ceiling in agricultural holdings.

Regulation No. 224, September 19, 1961, setting up procedures for redistributing land under the BAL and paying indemnifications.

Regulation No. 10, March 23, 1961, relating to the implementation of the registration of title to land.

Presidential Decree No. 131, 1961, setting up land reform committees.

Law No. 20, September 26, 1961, concerning the expropriation rights in land.

Regulation No. 7 of the Minister of Agrarian Affairs, September 7, 1961, concerning administration of land registration.

Regulation No. 2 of the Minister of Agriculture and Agrarian Affairs, September 1, 1962, concerning the conversion into new rights and registration of rights under the old land law.

Regulation No. 4 of the Minister of Agrarian Affairs, March 2, 1964, concerning the determination of shares in a sharecropping agreement.

Regulation No. 9, of the Minister of Home Affairs, December 6, 1965, relating to the right of Control (*hak penguasaan*) over land.

Regulation No. 6 of the Minister of Agrarian Affairs, 1965, concerning guidelines for land registration under Government Regulation No. 10, 1961.

Law No. 1 of 1961 concerning land control through indebtedness.

Emergency Law No. 3, 1963, updating Regulation No. 224 of 1961, regarding compensation payable on redistributed land.

Regulation No. 1 of Minister of Agrarian Affairs, January 5, 1966, concerning the registration of the right of use on state land and the so-called *hak pengelolaan.*

Regulation No. 3 of Directorate General of Agrarian Affairs and of Transmigration, February 13, 1967, relating to the utilization of land in transmigration areas and the grant of land rights.

Law No. 5, 1967, the Basic Forestry Law.

Decree No. 26, of Minister of Home Affairs, May 14, 1970, concerning confirmation of conversion and registration of Indonesian titles on land.

Regional Decree No. 1 of Governor of Jakarta, March 8, 1972, regarding urban infrastructure costs.

Law No. 3, 1972, the Basic Transmigration Law.

Regulation No. 6 of Minister of Home Affairs, 1972, relating to the delegation of authority for granting rights of land.

Instruction No. SD 16/10/3 of the Minister of Home Affairs, 1972, concerning the grant of land rights.

Presidential Decree No. 2, 1973, declaring the provinces of Jambi, Bengkulu, Lampung, South Sumatra, South Kalimantan, East Kalimantan, Central Kalimantan, South Sulawesi, Central Sulawesi, and Southeast Sulawesi as transmigration areas.

Regulation No. 5 of Minister of Home Affairs, 1973, concerning the procedure for granting land rights.

Regulation No. 42, of the Minister of Home Affairs, 1973, relating to the implementation of transmigration.

Joint Decree No. 91 of Minister of Home Affairs, 1973, concerning the implementation of the project for granting the right of land ownership and ownership certificates to settlers in transmigration areas.

Decree No. 140 of Minister of Home Affairs, 1973, stipulating the fees to be charged for the issue of ownership certificates (*hak milik*).

Decree No. 141 of Minister of Home Affairs, 1973, concerning the formulation of Advisory Committee on the Survey of land for Transmigrants.

Joint Instruction No. 22 of Minister of Home Affairs and Minister of Transmigration, 1974, concerning the formulation of a technical preparatory team for the transfer of transmigration projects.

Joint Instruction No. 25 of Minister of Home Affairs and Minister of Transmigration, 1974, concerning the transfer of certificates of land title and supervisory security of the property of settlers in transmigration areas.

Decree No. 1081 of Minister of Manpower, Transmigration and Cooperatives, 1974, regarding the organization tasks and working methods of the guidance and implementation bodies in transmigration areas.

Presidential Decree No. 29, 1974, concerning the formation of a body for the expansion of development in transmigration areas.

Regulation of No. 5 of 1974 Minister of Home Affairs, regarding urban development permission.

Regulation No. 15 of Minister of Home Affairs, 1975, clarifying expropriation procedure.

Regulation No. 4 of Minister of Home Affairs of 1980 regarding the management of urban development.

## Newspapers

*Daily*

Kompas
Sinar Harapan
Merdeka
Indonesian Times
Indonesian Observer
Jakarta Post

*Weekly*

Far Eastern Economic Review

# Index